DEAD POETS SOCIETY
the screenplay

Written by
Tom Schulman

HARVEST MOON PUBLISHING
SANTA MONICA

DEAD POETS SOCIETY: THE SCREENPLAY

The Script Publishing Project
Volume I Issue 1
March 2000

ISBN 1-929750-65-X
ISSN: 1524-2056

Published in the United States by Harvest Moon Publishing'
in association with The Writers Guild Foundation™

Harvest Moon Publishing'
P.O. Box 3332
Santa Monica, CA 90408
1-877-7-HARVEST
1-877-742-7837

The Writers Guild Foundation™
7000 W. 3rd Street
Los Angeles, CA 90048

www.harvestmoon.com
online@harvestmoon.com

ABOUT THE SCRIPT PUBLISHING PROJECT

WHY WE DO WHAT WE DO

Harvest Moon Publishing, in association with the Writers Guild Foundation, established the Script Publishing Project in 1998 in an effort to give the public greater access to the works of film and television writers. The Project enjoys the support of writers and studios and, through Harvest Moon, maintains the largest catalog of script titles of any publisher. In addition, Project sales raise funds for the Foundation, a non-profit corporation dedicated to preserving and promoting the craft of writing.

HOW WE DO WHAT WE DO

Unlike other publications, Harvest Moon scripts are published in their true format: pages are 8½ by 11 inches with the words printed on only one side of the page. These works are published just as the writers wrote them; they are not summarized or revised in any way. The principle behind the true format approach is that, like the layout of a poem, the way in which the words are set down on the page can dramatically affect the way a script is read.

TO FIND OUT MORE

Harvest Moon Publishing continues to add new film screenplays and television scripts to its catalog. To learn more about The Script Publishing Project or to receive an up-to-date list of available titles, contact:

HARVEST MOON PUBLISHING
P.O. BOX 3332
SANTA MONICA, CA 90408

1-877-7-HARVEST
1-877-742-7837

www.harvestmoon.com
online@harvestmoon.com

ABOUT THE WRITERS GUILD FOUNDATION

The Writers Guild Foundation was established in 1966 as a non-profit charitable corporation by a group of television and motion picture writers, members of the Writers Guild of America, west. The founding president was James. R. Webb.

THE FOUNDATION'S MISSION IS:

- to promote and encourage excellence in writing;
- to educate the public concerning the role of the writer in film and television;
- to preserve the work of film and television writers and thereby to create a significant historical resource for future generations;
- to encourage the further education of writers; and
- to promote communication between writers.

THE FOUNDATION'S CURRENT MAJOR PROGRAMS ARE:

- The James R. Webb Memorial Library, housing over 4,000 award nominated scripts and a reference collection of books, tapes and photographs related to writers and writing, and to the history of writers in Hollywood;

- *The Writer Speaks*, a series of oral history interviews on video with the great writers of film and television;

- *Words*, a short film highlighting and celebrating the writer's contribution to some of the great moments in motion pictures;

- Seminars and tributes, including its annual Career Achievement Award;

- An academic liaison program with schools and colleges;

- Conferences and international exchanges, including Words Into Pictures, a biennial forum for film and television writers.

TO FIND OUT MORE:

The Foundation's activities are funded by voluntary contributions from writers and industry friends. To learn more, or to find out how you can contribute, contact:

THE WRITERS GUILD FOUNDATION
(323) 782-4692

DEAD POETS SOCIETY

By

Tom Schulman

December 20, 1988

INT. WELTON ACADEMY DINING HALL, DAY. VARIOUS SHOTS.

CREDITS ROLL

On the left is a life-sized mural depicting a group of
young schoolboys looking up adoringly at a woman who
represents liberty. On the right is a mural showing young
men gathered around an industrialist in a corporate
boardroom. Between the murals stands a boy.

A blaring, MUSICAL SOUND starts and stops, interrupted by
the noise of pumping. A teacher takes the boy's picture.

On another wall is a full sized portrait of a 19th century
Scotsman in a kilt. In front of this, young boys carrying
banners, robed teachers, and several elderly men are
assembling into a processional formation. One of these
older gentlemen lights a candle.

Suddenly the music blasts forth in its full splendor. It
is a BAGPIPE. The bagpiper, in a kilt like the one in the
portrait, begins a processional march.

INT. THE CORRIDOR ADJACENT THE DINING ROOM, SAME.

The bagpiper enters a long slate and stone hallway. The
haunting timbre of his antiquated instrument reverberates
through the building. Momentarily he is followed by the
other processional marchers. He leads them down the
corridor and down a threshold staircase into:

INT. WELTON'S OLD, STONE CHAPEL, CONTINUOUS.

where three hundred high school aged boys - most of whom
wear black blazers - sit on either side of the central
aisle watching the procession move onto the dais in front.
Beside most of these boys are their parents.

VARIOUS ANGLES ON THE PROCESSION AND DAIS:

Watching the procession from the podium on the dais is
HEADMASTER GALE NOLAN, a man in his early sixties.

DOWN THE AISLE, FOUR SIXTEEN-YEAR-OLD BOYS CARRY BANNERS.

On each banner is emblazoned a different word. One reads
"TRADITION", another reads "HONOR", a third reads
"DISCIPLINE", the last reads "EXCELLENCE". Walking with
them are members of the school's faculty and a few elderly
alumni.

(CONTINUED)

CONTINUED:

                    NOLAN
          Ladies and Gentlemen, boys, the
          light of knowledge.

The older alumnus at the end of the procession reaches the
front where the seventh graders are seated. He lights the
nearest boy's candle with his, and the light of knowledge
ceremonially passes from old to young. The young boys
proceed to pass the flame from boy to boy.

                    NOLAN
          This year marks the one-hundredth
          year that Welton Academy has been
          in existence. One hundred years
          ago, in 1859, forty-one boys sat
          in this room and were asked the
          same question that now greets you
          at the start of each semester:
          Gentlemen, what are the four
          pillars?

All of the students stand at attention. Find TODD ANDERSON
sitting between his parents. Todd is sixteen, good looking
but he seems beaten down, lacking confidence, unhappy. He
wears a nametag and no Welton blazer. When the others
stand, Todd's parents nudge him. Todd stands. He watches
as the other students:

                    ALL THE BOYS IN UNISON
          Tradition! Honor! Discipline!
          Excellence!

All the boys sit. Todd sits too. All is silent again.

                    NOLAN
          In her first year, Welton Academy
          graduated five students. Last year
          we graduated fifty-one and over
          seventy-five percent of those went
          to the Ivy League!

Applause. During it we find KNOX OVERSTREET and CHARLIE
DALTON, both 16, and both in Welton blazers. Knox (sitting
between his parents) has curly hair, looks outgoing, is
short but well built. Charlie, also with his parents, has
a handsome yet friendly face. When Nolan mentions Ivy
League, both these boys fit the bill.

                    (CONTINUED)

CONTINUED: (2)

> NOLAN (CONT'D)
> This kind of accomplishment is the
> result of fervent dedication to
> the principles taught here. This
> is why you parents have been
> sending us your sons, and this is
> why we are the best preparatory
> school in the United States.

More applause. Sitting in the audience with his father is
NEIL PERRY. Like Knox and Charlie, he too looks the part
of the perfect Welton student. Beside him sits his stern
looking father, Mr. Perry.

> NOLAN (CONT'D)
> Gentlemen, at Welton you will work
> harder than you have ever worked
> in your lives, and your reward will
> be the success that all of us
> expect of you. Due to the
> retirement of our beloved English
> teacher Mr. Portius, I hope that
> you will all take the opportunity
> later to meet his replacement,
> Mr. John Keating, himself an
> honors graduate of this school,
> and who for the last several years
> has been teaching at the highly
> regarded Chester School in London.

MR. JOHN KEATING, sitting with the other faculty on the
dais, stands.

EXT. THE WELTON ACADEMY CHAPEL AND MAIN DRIVEWAY, DAY.

Welton Academy is a cluster of traditional weathered stone
buildings. The time is 1959 but at Welton this is
irrelevant. This school with its traditions is completely
isolated from the politics or trends of the outside world.

Mr. Nolan stands like a vicar outside his church, saying
hellos and good-byes to the students and their parents.

> NOLAN
> Ah, Mr. Anderson. You have some
> big shoes to fill young man. Your
> brother was one of our best.

> TODD
> (faint, almost inaudible)
> Thank you.

(CONTINUED)

CONTINUED:

Todd and his parents move on. Mr. Perry and Neil approach.

                    MR. PERRY
          Good to see you Mr. Nolan.

                    NOLAN
               (to Neil)
          We're expecting great things out
          of you this year, Mr. Perry.

                    NOLAN
          Thank you, Mr. Nolan.

                    MR. PERRY
          He won't disappoint us, right Neil?

                    NEIL
          No sir.

Nolan pats Neil's shoulder and moves on.

The seventh graders are saying goodbye to their parents.
Chins quiver. Young eyes hold back tears. Some boys sob.
For most of these young boys, this is the first time in
their lives that they will be away from their parents and
their homes and it is a devastating experience.

                    SEVENTH GRADER'S PARENT
          Don't cry.

EXT. WELTON CAMPUS - DAY

The Welton students walk toward their dorms. Neil Perry
approaches Todd Anderson and offers his handshake.

                    NEIL
          I hear we're going to be roommates.
          I'm Neil Perry.

                    TODD
               (softly)
          Todd. Anderson.

                    NEIL
          Why'd you leave Balincrest?

                    TODD
          My brother went here.

                    NEIL
          Oh, so you're that Anderson.

INT. THE JUNIOR DORM HALLWAY, CONTINUOUS.

Neil and Todd enter a confusion of students carrying
suitcases, etc. At the head of the hall, a school porter
minds a pile of luggage. Neil and Todd stop to look for
their suitcases. Neil finds his bags and moves on.

INT. THE WELTON JUNIOR CLASS DORMITORY ROOM, DAY.

Each small room contains two single beds, two closets, and
two desks. Neil enters carrying his suitcases. Richard
Cameron sticks in his head.

                    CAMERON
          Heard you got the new boy. Hear
          he's a stiff. Oops.

Todd Anderson walks in. Cameron ducks out. Todd has heard
Cameron's comment, but he ignores it. He puts his suitcase
on his bed and begins unpacking.

                    NEIL
          Don't mind Cameron. He's an
          asshole.

There is a knock on the door. Knox Overstreet, Charlie
Dalton, and Steven Meeks enter. Charlie speaks to Neil.

                    CHARLIE
          Hey, rumor has it you did summer
          school? Meeks, the door.

                    MEEKS
               (sarcastic)
          Yes sir!

Meeks closes the door.

                    NEIL
          Yeah, chemistry. My father thought
          I should get ahead.

                    CHARLIE
          Well, Meeks aced Latin and I didn't
          quite flunk English so if you want,
          we've got our study group.

                    NEIL
          Sure, but Cameron asked me too.
          Anybody mind including him?

                    CHARLIE
          What's his specialty, brown-nosing?

                    (CONTINUED)

CONTINUED:

Some chuckles.

> NEIL
> Hey, he's your roommate.

> CHARLIE
> That's not my fault.

Nobody is excited about Cameron but no one objects.

> MEEKS
> (to Todd)
> I don't think we've met. I'm Steven
> Meeks.

> TODD
> (shyly extending his hand)
> Todd. Anderson.

Knox and Charlie offer Todd handshakes.

> CHARLIE
> Charlie Dalton.

> KNOX
> Knox Overstreet.

Todd shakes their hands.

> NEIL
> Todd's brother is Jeffrey Anderson.

> CHARLIE
> Oh yeah. Sure. Valedictorian,
> National Merit Scholar...

Todd nods affirmative.

> MEEKS
> Well, welcome to "Hell"ton.

> CHARLIE
> It's every bit as hard as they say.
> Unless you're a genius like Meeks.

> MEEKS
> He flatters me so I'll help him
> with Latin.

> CHARLIE
> And English, and trig.

(CONTINUED)

5

CONTINUED: (2)

Meeks smiles. There is a knock on the door.

                    NEIL
          It's open.

Neil's father enters. Neil is surprised.

                    NEIL (CONT'D)
          Father. I thought you'd ... gone.

All the boys stand.

                    MEEKS, CHARLIE, KNOX
          Mr. Perry.

                    MR. PERRY
          Keep your seats, boys. How's it
          going?

                    THE BOYS
          Fine, sir. Thank you.

                    MR. PERRY
          Neil, I've decided that you're
          taking too many extracurricular
          activities. I've spoken to Mr.
          Nolan about it. You can work on
          the school annual next year.

                    NEIL
          But father, I'm the assistant
          editor.

                    MR. PERRY
          I'm sorry, Neil.

                    NEIL
          But father, it's not fair. I...

                    MR. PERRY
          Fellows, would you excuse us a
          minute?

Mr. Perry walks into the hall. Neil follows.

INT. THE JUNIOR DORMITORY HALLWAY - SAME

                    MR. PERRY
          I will not be disputed in public,
          do you understand me?

                              (CONTINUED)

CONTINUED:

                    NEIL
        Father, I wasn't disputing you.
        I...

                    MR. PERRY
        When you've finished medical school
        and you're on your own, you can
        do as you please. Until then, you
        will listen to me.

                    NEIL
        Yes sir. I'm sorry.

                    MR. PERRY
        You know what this means to your
        mother, don't you?

                    NEIL
        Yes sir.

Using the pressures of guilt and punishment, Mr. Perry is
the most subtle of bullies. Neil's resolve crumbles in
front of his authoritarian father. Neil fills the pause.

                    NEIL (CONT'D)
        You know me, always taking on too
        much.

                    MR. PERRY
        Good boy. Call us if you need
        anything.

He turns and walks off. Momentarily Charlie and Knox and
Meeks stick their heads out of Neil's room. They see a
chastened Neil.

                    CHARLIE
        Why doesn't he let you do what you
        want?

                    KNOX
        Yeah! Tell him off! It couldn't
        get any worse.

                    NEIL
        Oh that's rich. Like you tell your
        parents off, Mr. Future Lawyer and
        Mr. Future Banker!

                    CHARLIE
        Okay, so I don't like it any more
        than you do.

                    (CONTINUED)

CONTINUED: (2)

                         NEIL
          Then don't tell me how to talk to
          my father when you're the same way.
          All right?

                         KNOX
          All right. Jesus. What are you
          gonna do?

                         NEIL
          What I have to do. Screw the
          annual.

                         MEEKS
          I certainly wouldn't loose any
          sleep over it. It's just a bunch
          of people trying to impress Nolan.

                         NEIL
                    (bitterly)
          Screw it all. I don't give a damn
          about any of it.

Everyone is quiet, sensing Neil's disappointment. Finally,
Charlie breaks the silence.

                         CHARLIE
          I don't know about anyone else,
          but I could use a refresher in
          Latin. Eight o'clock in my room?

                         NEIL
          Sure.

Charlie calls back into Todd who is sitting at his desk,
putting things away.

                         CHARLIE
          You're welcome to join us Todd.

                         KNOX
          Yeah, come along.

                         TODD
          Thank you.

LONG SHOT, WELTON ACADEMY, SAME.

Welton Academy sits lonely and isolated in a valley in the
woods of Vermont. The setting is beautiful.

INT. THE WELTON DORM STAIRWELL, DAY.

Forty boys hurry down the stairs, creating a crush. MR. McALLISTER, a mid-60's teacher with a Scottish brogue tries to calm things down:

>   McALLISTER
>   Slow down, boys. Slow down you
>   miserable phalanx of pubescence!

INT. A CHEMISTRY CLASSROOM, DAY.

The classroom is a laboratory filled with flasks, etc. Neil, Todd, Knox, Charlie, Cameron, Meeks and other members of the junior class sit around the room. A bespectacled teacher stands in front, passing out thick textbooks.

>   CHEMISTRY TEACHER
>   In addition to the assignments in
>   the text, you will each pick three
>   lab experiments from the project
>   list and report on one every five
>   weeks. The first twenty problems at
>   the end of chapter one are due
>   tomorrow.

ANGLE ON CHARLIE DALTON as the thick textbooks arrive at his desk. He shoots a disbelieving glance at Knox Overstreet who can only acknowledge with a shake of his head. Todd takes his books without reacting.

INT. LATIN CLASS, DAY.

The same students sit before the Latin teacher. It is Mr. McAllister, the teacher with the Scottish brogue. He declines a Latin noun:

>   LATIN TEACHER (McALLISTER)
>   Agricola, agricolae, agricolas,
>   Agricolas, agricolatis,
>   agricolatus ....

INT. A MATHEMATICS CLASS - DAY

Mathematical charts hang on the walls. The elderly bald teacher (the one from Nolan's doorway), Dr. Hager, passes out books. The students' workload is huge.

(CONTINUED)

CONTINUED:

                    HAGER
          Your study of trigonometry requires
          absolute precision. Anyone failing
          to turn in any homework assignment
          will be penalized one point off
          his final grade. Let me urge you
          now not to test me on this point.

INT. ENGLISH CLASSROOM - DAY

The junior students--Todd, Neil, Knox, Charlie, Cameron,
Meeks and some of the others we've seen--enter. They are
loaded down with books and look weary. Standing in the
anteroom behind the teacher's desk, peering out at the
boys is JOHN KEATING, the teacher we glimpsed earlier. He
wears a collared shirt, tie, no jacket.

The boys take seats and settle in. The students start to
shuffle uncomfortably. Finally Keating enters and begins
strolling the aisles. He walks out of the room.

The boys look at each other, not knowing what to do.
Keating sticks his head back into the room.

                    KEATING
          Well, come on.

He exits again. After a moment the confused boys get up to
follow.

INT. THE WELTON OAK PANELED HONOR ROOM - DAY

The walls are lined with class pictures dating back into
the 1800s. School trophies of every description fill
trophy cases and shelves. Keating leads the students in,
then faces the class.

                    KEATING
          "Oh Captain, My Captain." Who knows
          where that's from? Anybody?

No one raises a hand.

                    KEATING
          It was written by a poet named Walt
          Whitman about Mr. Abraham Lincoln.
          In this class you may refer to me
          as either Mr. Keating, or - if you
          want to be more daring - Oh
          Captain, My Captain.
                    (more)

                                        (CONTINUED)

CONTINUED:

>   KEATING (Cont'd)
>   So that I become the source of as
>   few rumors as possible, let me tell
>   you that yes, I too attended Helton
>   and survived and no, at that time
>   I was not the intellectual giant
>   you see before you today. In fact,
>   I was the intellectual equivalent
>   of a ninety eight pound weakling.
>   I would go to the beach and people
>   would kick copies of Byron in my
>   face.

Keating looks at his roll.

>   KEATING
>   Mister... Pitts. An unfortunate
>   name. Where are you Mister Pitts?

Pitts raises a hand.

>   KEATING
>   Open your text, Pitts, to page 542
>   and read for us the first stanza
>   of the poem.

Pitts looks through his book. He finds the poem.

>   PITTS
>   "To The Virgins to Make Much of
>   Time"?

>   KEATING
>   That's the one. Somewhat
>   appropriate isn't it?

Giggles from the class. Pitts reads.

>   PITTS
>   "Gather ye rosebuds while ye may
>   Old time is still a flying And this
>   same flower that smiles today
>   Tomorrow will be dying."

>   KEATING
>   "Gather ye rosebuds while ye may."
>   The Latin term for that sentiment
>   is "Carpe Diem." Anyone know what
>   that means?

>   MEEKS
>   Carpe Diem... seize the day.

(CONTINUED)

CONTINUED: (2)

                    KEATING
          Very good, Mr....?

                    MEEKS
          Meeks.

                    KEATING
          Another unusual name. Seize the
          day. Gather ye rosebuds while ye
          may. Why does the poet write these
          lines?

                    CHARLIE
          Because he's in a hurry?

                    KEATING
          Because we're food for worms, lads!
          Because we're only going to
          experience a limited number of
          springs, summers, and falls. One
          day, hard as it is to believe, each
          and every one of us is going to
          stop breathing, turn cold, and die!
          Now I want you to walk over and
          peruse the faces of the boys who
          attended this school sixty or
          seventy years ago. Don't be timid,
          come look at them.

The boys - Todd, Neil, Knox, Meeks, etc. go over to the
class pictures that line the honor room walls.

ANGLES ON VARIOUS PICTURES ON THE WALLS. Faces of young
men stare at us from out of the past.

                    KEATING
          They're not that different than
          any of you, are they? Hope in
          their eyes, just like you. Full
          of hormones just like you. They
          believed themselves destined for
          wonderful things. Well, where are
          those smiles now, boys? What of
          that hope?

THE BOYS are staring at the pictures, sobered by what
Keating is saying.

                         (CONTINUED)

14.

CONTINUED: (3)

                    KEATING (CONT'D)
          Did most of them not wait until it
          was too late before making their
          lives into even one iota of what
          they were capable? In chasing the
          almighty deity of success did they
          not squander their boyhood dreams?
          Most of those gentlemen are
          fertilizing daffodils! However,
          if you get very close, boys, you
          can hear them whisper their legacy
          to you. Go ahead, lean in. Hear
          it?
                    (loud whisper)
          "Carpe... CARPE... Carpe Diem,
          lads. Seize the day. Make your
          lives extraordinary."

Todd, Neil, Knox, Charlie, Cameron, Meeks, Pitts all stare
into the pictures on the wall. All are lost in thought.

EXT. THE WELTON CAMPUS - DAY

The class files out of the honor room. Todd, Neil, Knox,
Charlie, Cameron, Meeks, and Pitts walk together, books in
hand. All thinking about what just happened in class.

                    PITTS
          Weird.

                    NEIL
          But different.

                    KNOX
          Spooky if you ask me.

                    CAMERON
          You think he'll test us on that
          stuff?

                    CHARLIE
          Oh come on, Cameron, don't you get
          anything?

                    CAMERON
          What?

INT. THE WELTON SHOWER ROOM, DAY.

                    (CONTINUED)

CONTINUED:

Boys are dressing, undressing, moving back and forth to
the showers, etc. DOLLY IN SLOWLY on Todd who is sitting
on a bench, slowly undressing, lost in thought.

                    MEEKS
          How about a trig study group?
          Right after dinner.

                    VARIOUS BOYS
          Good by me. Sure. Great.

The Gym Master strolls through, monitoring the activity.

                    GYM MASTER
          Pick up the soap, Harrison. Move
          out, boys. And that means you,
          Daulton.

                    KNOX
          I can't make it. I got a sign-out
          to have dinner at the Danburrys'
          house.

                    PITTS
          Who are the Danburrys?

                    CAMERON
          Big alums. How'd you pull that?

                    KNOX
          They're friends of my dad.
          Probably in their nineties or
          something.

                    NEIL
          Listen, anything's better than
          mystery meat.

                    CHARLIE
          I'll second that.

Neil approaches Todd who is now deep in thought.

                    NEIL
          Want to come to the study group?

                    TODD
          Thanks but... I'd better do
          history.

INT. TODD AND NEIL'S DORM ROOM - LATE AFTERNOON

Todd takes out his notebook and opens his history book. He
stares at his notebook for a moment, then writes "SEIZE
THE DAY" in big letters. He looks at the words that he's
written, sighs, tears the page off, then plunges into his
homework.

INT. THE HONOR ROOM, DUSK

Knox stands around, looking at the pictures on the wall.
Dr. Hager enters carrying car keys.

                    DR. HAGER
          Ready, Overstreet.

They exit.

EXT. THE WELTON CAMPUS - DUSK - WIDE SHOT

The autumnal colors are muted by the onset of nightfall.
Old Dr. Hager drives the school "woody" station wagon out
of the campus.

EXT. WELTON VILLAGE - DUSK -

The woody drives through the sleepy village of Welton.

EXT./INT. A LARGE MANSION - DUSK

Knox walks to the door of the home and rings the bell.
After a moment, the door is opened by a beautiful eighteen
year old girl. Soft glowing eyes, athletic figure under
a tennis dress, this girl is stunning. Knox stands looking
at her, absolutely THUNDERSTRUCK. Finally he manages to
speak.

                    KNOX
          Hi.

                    GIRL
          Hi.

                    KNOX
          I, er...

                    GIRL
          Are you here to see Chet?

                    KNOX
          Mrs. Danburry?

                    (CONTINUED)

CONTINUED:

A middle-aged woman sticks her head around the girl.

                    WOMAN (MRS. DANBURRY)
          I have it dear. Knox. Come in. I'm
          Janette Danburry.

Knox enters and watches as the girl goes hurrying
upstairs. Mrs. Danburry leads Knox towards the library.
JOE DANBURRY a sharp looking man of about 40, well
dressed, friendly, greets Knox at the library door.

                    JOE DANBURRY
          Knox, come in. Joe Danburry.

                    KNOX
              (looking after the girl but to
               Mr. Danburry)
          Nice to meet you.

                    JOE DANBURRY
          You're the spitting image of your
          father. How is he?

                    KNOX
          Great. Just did a big case for GM.

                    JOE DANBURRY
          Ah. I know where you're headed.
          Like father like son, eh?

Knox smiles, trying to pay attention to Mr. Danburry, but
his attention is still on the girl upstairs.

INT. THE JUNIOR CLASS LOUNGE - NIGHT

The dorm is quiet. Neil, Cameron, Meeks, Charlie and Pitts
are gathered studying math. As they do, Pitts and Meeks
work to assemble a small crystal radio. Knox, looking
shell-shocked, shuffles into the lobby.

                    CHARLIE
          How was dinner?

                    KNOX
          Terrible. Awful! I met the most
          beautiful girl I've ever seen in
          my life!

                    NEIL
          Are you crazy? What's wrong with
          that?

                         (CONTINUED)

CONTINUED:

                    KNOX
          She's practically engaged to Chet
          Danburry. Mr. Mondo Jocko himself.

                    PITTS
          Too bad.

                    KNOX
          It's worse than too bad, Pitts,
          it's a tragedy! Why does she have
          to be in love with a jerk?

                    PITTS
          All the good ones go for jerks,
          you know that. Forget her. Take
          out your trig book and figure out
          problem twelve.

                    KNOX
          I can't just forget her, Pitts.
          And I certainly can't think about
          math!

Hager enters.

                    HAGER
          Five minutes, gentlemen.

The boys start to shuffle out.

                    KNOX
          You really think I should forget
          her?

                    PITTS
          You have another choice?

                    CHARLIE
             (exiting)
          Did you see her naked?

                    KNOX
          That's not funny, Daulton.

EXT. WELTON CAMPUS - MORNING

The Welton bagpiper marches on the lawn, practicing.
Students emerge from their dorms and head to breakfast.

INT. KEATING'S ENGLISH CLASS - DAY

Keating sits in a chair behind the teacher's desk.

                    KEATING
          Boys, open your Pritchard texts
          to page 21 of the introduction.
          Mr. Perry, kindly read aloud the
          first paragraph of the preface
          entitled "Understanding Poetry."

The boys find the page in their texts. Neil reads.

                    NEIL
          Understanding Poetry by Dr. J.
          Evans Pritchard, Ph.D. To fully
          understand poetry, we must first
          be fluent with it's meter, rhyme,
          and figures of speech, then ask
          two questions: 1)how artfully has
          the objective of the poem been
          rendered and 2)how important is
          that objective? Question 1) rates
          the poem's perfection; question
          2) rates its importance; and once
          these questions have been answered,
          determining the poem's greatness
          becomes a relatively simple matter.
          If the poem's score for perfection
          is plotted on the horizontal of
          a graph and its importance is
          plotted on the vertical, then
          calulating the total area of the
          poem yields the measure of it's
          greatness. A sonnet by Byron might
          score high on the vertical but only
          average on the horizontal. A
          Shakespearean sonnet, on the other
          hand, would score high both
          horizontally and vertically,
          yielding a massive total area,
          thereby revealing the poem to be
          truly great.

As Neil reads Keating goes to the blackboard and draws a
graph. He demonstrates by lines and shading how the
Shakespeare poem would overwhelm the Byron.

                    NEIL (CONT'D)
          As you proceed through the poetry
          in this book, practice this rating
          method. As your ability to evaluate
          poems in this manner grows, so will
          your enjoyment and understanding
          of poetry.

                         (CONTINUED)

CONTINUED:

Neil stops. Keating pauses a moment to let this lesson
sink in.

>   KEATING
>   Excrement! That's what I think of
>   Dr. J. Evans Pritchard. Now I want
>   you to rip that page out of your
>   books. Go on, rip out the entire
>   page! I want this garbage on the
>   trash heap where it belongs!

The boys are tentative. Does Keating mean this?

>   KEATING
>   Go ahead, rip it out. Rip it out!

Charlie Daulton rips out the page.

>   KEATING
>   Thank you mister Daulton. Come on,
>   make a clean tear. In fact, rip out
>   the entire introduction. I want
>   nothing left of it! Dr. J. Evans
>   Pritchard you are disgraceful!

The other boys begin ripping out pages from their books,
having a good time of it. Keating goes into the anteroom
and picks up the trashcan.

INT. McALLISTER'S CLASSROOM - DAY

Mr. McAllister, the Scottish Latin teacher, exits his room
and walks across the hall to Keating's classroom. He peeks
in the door window and sees boys ripping pages out of
their books. Alarmed, McAllister opens the door and enters
Keating's room.

INT. KEATING'S CLASSROOM - SAME

>   McALLISTER
>   What the hell is going on in
>   here!...

>   KEATING (O.S.)
>   I want to hear more ripping!

Keating exits the anteroom. McAllister sees him.

>   McALLISTER
>   Sorry, I didn't think you were in
>   here, Mr. Keating.

                    (CONTINUED)

CONTINUED:

                    KEATING
          Well, I am.

                    McALLISTER
          So I see. Sorry.

                    KEATING
          Anytime.

Baffled and embarrassed, McAllister exits. Keating strides
back to the front of the room.

                    KEATING
          This is battle, boys. War! And the
          casualties could be your hearts and
          souls. Now you will learn what this
          school wants you to learn in my
          class, however, if I do my job
          properly, you will also learn a
          great deal more. You will learn to
          think for yourselves. You will
          learn to savor language and words
          because, no matter what anyone
          tells you gentlemen, words and
          ideas have the power to change the
          world. Now, Mr. Pitts may argue
          that nineteenth-century literature
          has nothing to do with business
          school or medical school. He thinks
          we should study our J. Evans
          Pritchard, learn our rhyme and
          meter, and quietly go about our
          business of achieving other
          ambitions.

Pitts smilingly shakes his head as if to say "Who me?"

                    KEATING
               (defiant whisper)
          Well, I say drivel. One reads
          poetry because he is a member of
          the human race and the human race
          is filled with passion! Medicine,
          law, banking--these are necessary
          to sustain life-- but poetry,
          romance, love, beauty! These are
          what we stay alive for! I quote
          from Whitman: "Oh me, Oh life of
          the questions of these recurring.
          Of the endless trains of the
          faithless, of cities filled with
          the foolish...
               (more)
                              (CONTINUED)

22

CONTINUED: (2)

                    KEATING (Cont'd)
          What good amid these O me, O life?
          Answer: That you are here-- That
          life exists and identity, That the
          powerful play goes on, and you may
          contribute a verse."

Keating pauses. The class sits, taking this in.

                    KEATING (CONT'D)
                 (awestruck tone)
          "That the powerful play goes on,
          and you may contribute a verse."

Keating waits a long moment.

                    KEATING (CONT'D)
          What will your verse be?

CLOSE ON the faces of NEIL, KNOX, CHARLIE, MEEKS, CAMERON,
PITTS, and finally TODD as they contemplate this question.

INT. THE WELTON DINING ROOM - DAY

On the dais in the front of the room is the teachers'
dining table. Below them are the students' tables. Mr.
McAllister sits to Keating's right.

                    McALLISTER
          Quite an interesting class you had
          today, Mr. Keating.

                    KEATING
          Sorry if I shocked you.

                    McALLISTER
          No need to apologize. It was quite
          fascinating, misguided though it
          was.

                    KEATING
          YOU think so?

                    McALLISTER (CONT'D)
          You take a big risk encouraging
          them to be artists, John. When they
          realize that they're not Rembrandts
          or Shakespeares or Mozarts, they'll
          hate you for it.

                    KEATING
          Not artists, George, free thinkers.

                    (CONTINUED)

23

CONTINUED:

                    McALLISTER
          Ah, free thinkers at seventeen?

                    KEATING
          I hardly pegged you as a cynic.

                    McALLISTER
          Not a cynic. A realist! Show me the
          heart unfettered by foolish dreams
          and I'll show you a happy man.

He chews a bite.

                    (EATING)
          Only in their dreams can men be
          truly free. 'Twas always thus and
          always thus will be.

                    McALLISTER
          Tennyson?

                    KEATING
          Keating.

McAllister laughs.

ANOTHER ANGLE - THE DINING ROOM - SAME

Todd, Knox, Charlie, Cameron, Pitts, and Meeks sit at a
table eating. Neil enters and joins them.

                    NEIL
          I found his senior annual in the
          library.

Neil opens the annual and reads.

                    NEIL (CONT'D)
          "Captain of the soccer team, editor
          of the annual, Cambridge bound,
          Man most likely to do anything,
          Thigh man, Dead Poets Society."

Hands grab the old annual away from Neil.

                    CHARLIE
          Thigh man? Mr. "K" was a hell-
          raiser.

                    KNOX
          What is the Dead Poets Society?

                    (CONTINUED)

24

CONTINUED: (2)

                    MEEKS
          Any group picture in the annual?

                    NEIL
          Nothing. No other mention of it.

                    CHARLIE
          Nolan.

Mr. Nolan approaches the boys' table. Under the table,
Cameron insistently hands the annual to Todd. Todd looks
at Cameron, then takes it.

EXT. THE CAMPUS - LATER

Keating walks across the school lawn wearing his sport
coat and a scarf, carrying his books. Knox, Charlie,
Meeks, Pitts, Neil, Cameron, and Todd approach him.

                    NEIL
          Mr. Keating?... Sir?... Oh Captain,
          My Captain.

Keating stops and turns.

                    KEATING
          Gentlemen.

                    NEIL
          What was the Dead Poets Society?

Keating reacts.

                    NEIL
          I was just looking in an old annual
          and...

                    KEATING
          Nothing wrong with research.

He takes the annual and looks at it. He laughs at the
picture of himself.   The boys wait.

                    NEIL
          But what was it?

Keating checks around to be sure they are unwatched.

                    (CONTINUED)

25

CONTINUED:

                    KEATING
          A secret organization. I don't know
          how the present administration
          would look upon it but I doubt the
          reaction would be favorable. Can
          you keep a secret?

An instant sea of nods.

                    KEATING
          The Dead Poets was a society
          dedicated to sucking the marrow out
          of life. That phrase is by Thoreau
          and was invoked at every meeting. A
          small group of us would meet at the
          old Indian cave and there we would
          take turns reading Shelley,
          Thoreau, Whitman, the biggies - and
          in the enchantment of the moment
          let it work its magic on us.

                    KNOX
          You mean it was a bunch of guys
          sitting around reading poetry?

                    KEATING
                (amused)
          Both sexes participated, Mr.
          Overstreet. And we didn't simply
          read... we let it drip from our
          tongues like honey. Women swooned,
          spirits soared... Gods were
          created, gentlemen. Not a bad way
          to spend an evening, eh?

The boys laugh. Keating hands back the annual.

                    KEATING
          Burn this. Especially my picture.

Keating exits. The boys stand watching. Neil turns to
them.

                    NEIL
          I say we go tonight. Everybody in?

                    PITTS
          Where is this cave he's talking
          about?

                    NEIL
          Beyond the stream. I think I know.

                    (CONTINUED)

26

CONTINUED: (2)

                         PITTS
            That's miles.

                         CAMERON
            Sounds boring to me.

                         CHARLIE
            Don't come.

                         CAMERON
            You know how many demerits we're
            talking?

                         CHARLIE
            So don't goddamn come! Please.

                         CAMERON
            All I'm saying is we have to be
            careful. We can't get caught.

                         CHARLIE
                 (sarcastic)
            Well, no shit, Sherlock.

                         NEIL
            Who's in?

                         CHARLIE
            I'm in.

                         CAMERON
            Me too.

Neil looks at Knox, Pitts, and Meeks.

                         PITTS
            Well...

                         CHARLIE
            Oh come on, Pitts...

                         MEEKS
            His grades are hurting, Charlie.

                         NEIL
            Then you can help him.

                         PITTS
            What is this, a midnight study
            group?

                              (CONTINUED)

27

CONTINUED: (3)

                    NEIL
          Forget it, Pitts, you're coming.
          Meeks, your grades hurting too?

Laughter.

                    MEEKS
          All right. I'll try anything <u>once</u>.

                    CHARLIE
          Except sex.

More laughter. Meeks blushes.

                    CAMERON
          I'm in as long as we're careful.

                    CHARLIE
          Knox?

                    KNOX
          I don't know. I don't get it.

                    CHARLIE
          Come on. It'll help you get Chris.

                    KNOX
          It will? How do you figure?

                    CHARLIE
          "Women swoon!"

                    KNOX
          But why?

The group walk off. Knox holds, then follows.

                    KNOX (CONT'D)
          Why do they swoon?! Charlie, tell
          me why they swoon!

A bell rings. Dr. Hager watches as Knox moves off after
the others. Todd remains behind. No one asked Todd and he
moves off by himself.

INT. THE STUDY HALL - LATE AFTERNOON

Students study. Neil sits near Todd.

                    (CONTINUED)

28

CONTINUED:

> NEIL
> (hushed voice)
> Listen, I'm inviting you. You can't
> expect everybody to think of you
> all the time. Nobody knows you.

> TODD
> Thanks but it's not a question of
> that.

> NEIL
> What is it then?

> TODD
> I... I just don't want to come.

> NEIL
> But why? Don't you understand what
> Keating is saying? Don't you want
> to do something about it?

> TODD
> Yes. But...

> NEIL
> But what? Goddamn it, tell me.

> TODD
> I don't want to read.

> NEIL
> What?

> TODD
> Keating said everybody took turns
> reading. I don't want to do it.

> NEIL
> God, you really have a problem,
> don't you? How can it hurt you to
> read? I mean isn't that what this
> is all about? Expressing yourself?

> TODD
> Neil, I can't explain it. I just
> don't want to do it.

Neil is peeved by this attitude. They sit in silence a
moment.

> NEIL
> What if you didn't have to read?
> What if you came and just listened?

(CONTINUED)

29

CONTINUED: (2)

> TODD
> That's not the way it works. If I
> join, the guys will want me to
> read.

> NEIL
> I know, but what if they said you
> didn't have to?

> TODD
> You mean ask them? Neil, it's
> embarrassing!

> NEIL
> No it's not. Just wait here.

Neil moves away.

> TODD
> Neil!

Neil is off before Todd can stop him. Todd sits in
frustration.

INT. THE DORM HALLWAY - NIGHT

Boys move about in pajamas carrying towels. Neil talks in
low tones with Charlie and Knox, then walks to Todd.

> NEIL
> You're in.

INT. TODD AND NEIL'S ROOM - NIGHT

Neil enters, tosses his towel aside, then notices
something on his desk. He pauses then picks it up. It is
an old, well-worn, dog-eared Poetry anthology. Neil opens
it.

On the inside cover in longhand is written:

> "J. KEATING"

Beneath that is scrawled: "Dead Poets".

INT. THE DORM - LATE NIGHT

Old Dr. Hager, the resident dorm marshal, putters in his
room, door ajar, making tea. He senses something and moves
to his door. He looks up and down the empty corridor.

30

INT./EXT VARIOUS PARTS OF THE SCHOOL - NIGHT

The boys' shadows and occasional flicker of a flashlight
pass walls, paintings and statuary as the boys leave the
school. The school hunting-dog comes up and barks at the
boys. Pitts drops some dog biscuits on the ground and this
keeps the dog occupied.

EXT. THE SCHOOL GROUNDS - NIGHT

The stars are out and the wind is blowing. A SERIES OF
SHOTS show the boys crossing the campus.

EXT. THE WELTON WOODS AND STREAM - NIGHT

The boys make their way through the eerie forest searching
for the cave. They reach the bank of the stream and begin
looking for an appropriate spot amongst the tree roots and
erosion. Charlie suddenly looms out of the cave entrance.

                    CHARLIE
          Yaa, I'm a dead poet!

                    MEEKS
               (frightened)
          Ahh!
               (then recovering)
          Eat it, Dalton!

                    CHARLIE
          This is it, guys. Over here!

                    SHORT DISSOLVE TO:

INT. THE CAVE - A BIT LATER

A newly lit fire comes to life. The boys stand around the
cave coughing.

                    NEIL
          Forget the fire.

Feet stomp out the fire. The smoke clears. Neil stands
before the group, holding the book Keating left in his
room.

                    (CONTINUED)

31

CONTINUED:

                         NEIL
          I hereby reconvene the Welton
          Chapter of the Dead Poets Society.
          These meetings will be conducted
          by myself and by the rest of the
          new initiates now present. Todd
          Anderson, because he prefers not
          to read, will keep minutes of the
          meetings.

Todd is unhappy with this role but he tries not to show it.

                         NEIL (CONT'D)
          I will now read the traditional
          opening message from society member
          Henry David Thoreau.

Neil opens the book that Keating left him and reads:

                         NEIL (CONT'D)
          "I went to the woods because I
          wanted to live deliberately." "I
          wanted to live deep and suck out
          all the marrow of life!"

                         CHARLIE
          I'll second that.

                         NEIL
          "To put the rout all that was not
          life." "And not, when I came to
          die, discover that I had not
          lived." Mr. Keating's marked other
          passages for us to read.

                         CHARLIE
          Hold on guys, let's take a break.
          Meeks, lay your coat down. I want
          to see what everybody's brought.

                         MEEKS
          Yes sir.

Meeks puts his coat on the ground and the boys lay out
food - apples, raisins, rolls, etc. Someone puts down half
a roll.

                         CHARLIE
          Who put down half a roll?

                         KNOX
                    (full mouth)
          I'm eating the other half.

                         (CONTINUED)

32

CONTINUED: (2)

Pitts has been flipping through the volume of poetry.

                    PITTS
          Listen to this: "Here lies my wife:
          so let her lie. Now she's at
          rest... And so am I!"

                    MEEKS
          And listen to this...

                    CHARLIE
          Wait a minute. You want to hear a
          real poem. Put that away.

                    MEEKS
          What do you have there, Charlie?

Charlie opens up a Playboy pinup. It's a voluptuous
foldout of a half-naked model.

                    BOYS
          Whoa! Where did you get that?

Charlie clears his throat.

                    CHARLIE
               (reads)
          "Teach me to love? Go teach thyself
          more wit. For I am chief professor
          of it. The gods of love, if such a
          thing there be. May learn to love
          from me."

                    NEIL
          Whoa, did you write that?

                    CHARLIE
          Abraham Cowley.

He flashes the pinup at them. The boys laugh. Neil looks
through the book.

                    NEIL
          Listen to this...
               (reads)
          "Come my friends, 'tis not too late
          to seek a newer world.... For our
          purpose holds to sail beyond the
          sunset. And though we are not now
               (more)

                    (CONTINUED)

33

CONTINUED: (3)

                    NEIL (Cont'd)
          that same strength which in old
          days moved earth and heaven, that
          which we are, we are: One equal
          temper of heroic hearts, made weak
          by time and fate, but strong in
          will, To strive, to seek, to find
          but not to yield."

Meeks reads from the book.

                    MEEKS
          "Then I saw the congo creeping
          through the black, Cutting through
          the jungle with a golden track."
                    (repeats)

The boys begin moving to the rhythm of this poem. Someone
beats on his flashlight. Soon the whole group is dancing
around the fire as Meeks reads these lines over and over.

EXT. THE CAVE AND WOODS, NIGHT.

The boys clown and dance, getting steadily wilder and more
ridiculous in their gestures, making jungle noises,
beating their own and each others' legs and heads, etc.
Charlie leads the boys into the night.

                    DISSOLVE TO:

INT. KEATING'S CLASSROOM - DAY

Keating paces around the class, teaching.

                    KEATING
          A man is not very tired, he is
          exhausted. Don't use very sad, use-

Keating snaps his fingers and points to Knox.

                    KEATING
          Come on Overstreet, you twirp.

                    KNOX
          ...Morose?

                    KEATING
          Good! Language was invented for one
          reason, boys--

He snaps his fingers again and points to Neil.

                    (CONTINUED)

34

CONTINUED:

                    NEIL
          To communicate?

                    KEATING
          No. To woo women. And, in that
          endeavor, laziness will not do. It
          also won't do in your essays.

Keating paces then suddenly leaps onto his desk.

                    KEATING
          Why do I stand up here?

                    CHARLIE
          To feel taller?

                    KEATING
          I stand on my desk to remind myself
          that we must constantly force
          ourselves to look at things
          differently. The world looks
          different from up here. If you
          don't believe it, stand up here and
          try it. All of you. Take turns.

Keating jumps off. The boys go to the front of the room
and a few at a time take turns standing on Keating's desk.
As they do, Keating strolls up and down the aisles.

                    KEATING
          If you're sure about something,
          force yourself to think about it
          another way, even if you know it's
          wrong or silly. When you read,
          don't consider only what the author
          thinks, but take time to consider
          what you think. You must strive to
          find your own voice, boys, and the
          longer you wait to begin, the less
          likely you are to find it at all.
          Thoreau said "Most men lead lives
          of quiet desperation." Why be
          resigned to that? Risk walking new
          ground. Now.

Keating goes to the door. He looks at the class, then
flashes the room lights on and off over and over. He makes
a noise like crashing thunder.

                                        (CONTINUED)

35

CONTINUED: (2)

                    KEATING (CONT'D)
          In addition to your essays, I want
          you each to write a poem --
          something your own -- to be
          delivered aloud in class. See you
          Monday.

He exits. Momentarily, he pops his head back in.

                    KEATING (CONT'D)
               (impish grin)
          And don't think I don't know this
          assignment scares you to death, Mr.
          Anderson, you mole.

The class laughs. Todd forces a hint of a smile.

INT./EXT. WELTON CAMPUS, AFTERNOON - <u>VARIOUS LOCATIONS</u> - MONTAGE

Pitts and Meeks climb up the inside of the bell tower that
sits atop the Welton Chapel. They affix Pitts' crystal
radio antenna to the chapel cross. Momentarily, they tune
in a rock 'n roll station.

                    PITTS
          Radio Free America.

The music dissolves into static. They jiggle the radio in
frustration.

Some of the Welton students fence across the green.

Down at the lake, the Welton crew team is practicing. Mr.
Nolan sits in a rowboat, smoking a pipe, coaching.

School grounds -- on a bike, Knox approaches the Welton
gates. He checks over his shoulder to make sure he's not
been seen, then pedals furiously to the outside.

Countryside -- Knox pedals hard, determined to get where
he's going.

Welton Village -- Knox bikes through.

Knox comes to RIDGEWAY HIGH SCHOOL. He stops. He sees:

Beyond a fence buses stand while students board. Into one
bus file members of the uniformed marching band,
practicing their drum rolls, etc. Into another bus go the
football players. Into a third bus go the cheerleaders,
among them Chris.

                    (CONTINUED)

36

CONTINUED:

Knox watches Chris longingly. Before she boards her bus, she rushes up and gives Chet - carrying his football gear - a peck on the lips. Chet holds her to him and she giggles, then she runs and climbs into the cheerleaders' bus.

Knox gets back on his bike and pedals away.

INT. TODD AND NEIL'S ROOM - AFTERNOON

Todd sits at his bed, a pad of paper beside him. He starts to write something then scratches it out in frustration. The door opens. Neil enters, looking like he's just seen God.

                    NEIL
          I've found it.

                    TODD
          Found what?

                    NEIL
          What I want to do! Right now.
          What's really inside of me.

He hands Todd a piece of paper. Todd reads it.

                    TODD
          "A Midsummer Night's Dream." What
          is it?

                    NEIL
          A play, dummy.

                    TODD
          I know that. What's it got to do
          with you?

                    NEIL
          They're putting it on at Henley
          Hall. See, open try-outs.

                    TODD
          So?

                    NEIL
          So I'm gonna act! Ever since I can
          remember I've wanted to try it.
          Last summer I even tried to go to
          summer stock auditions but of
          course my father wouldn't let me.

                    (CONTINUED)

37

CONTINUED:

                         TODD
          And now he will?

                         NEIL
          Hell no, but that's not the point.
          The point is for the first time in
          my whole goddamned life, I know
          what I want, and for the first time
          I'm gonna do it whether my father
          wants me to or not! Carpe diem,
          goddamn it!

Neil picks up the play and reads a couple of lines aloud.
They delight him. He clenches his fists in the air with
joy.

                         TODD
          Neil, how are you gonna be in a
          play if your father won't let you?

                         NEIL
          First I gotta get the part, then
          I'll worry about that.

                         TODD
          Won't he kill you if you don't let
          him know you're auditioning?

                         NEIL
          As far as I'm concerned, he won't
          have to know about any of it.

                         TODD
          Come on, that's impossible.

                         NEIL
          Nothing's impossible.

                         TODD
          Why don't you ask him first? Maybe
          he'll say yes.

                         NEIL
          That's a laugh. If I don't ask, at
          least I won't be disobeying him.

                         TODD
          But if he said no before then...

                         (CONTINUED)

38

CONTINUED: (2)

                    NEIL
          Jesus Christ, whose side are you
          on? I haven't even gotten the part
          yet. Can't I enjoy the idea even
          for a little while?

Todd turns back to his work. Neil sits on the bed and
starts reading the play.

                    NEIL (CONT'D)
          By the way, there's a meeting this
          afternoon. You coming?

                    TODD
               (blase)
          I guess.

Neil puts down his play and looks at Todd.

                    NEIL
          None of what Mr. Keating has to say
          means anything to you, does it?

                    TODD
          What is that supposed to mean?

                    NEIL
          Being in the club means being
          stirred up by things. You look
          about as stirred up as a cesspool.

                    TODD
          You want me out...is that what
          you're saying?

                    NEIL
          No, I want you in. But being in
          means you gotta do something. Not
          just say you're in.

                    TODD
               (turns angrily)
          Listen Neil, I appreciate your
          interest in me but I'm not like
          you. When you say things, people
          pay attention. People follow you.
          I'm not like that.

                    NEIL
          Why not? Don't you think you could
          be?

                    (CONTINUED)

39

CONTINUED: (3)

                    TODD
          No! I don't know. I'll probably
          never know. The point is, there's
          nothing you can do about it so butt
          out, all right? I can take care of
          myself just fine. All right?

                    NEIL
          Er... No.

                    TODD
          No? What do you mean 'no'?

                    NEIL
               (shrugs matter-of-factly)
          No.

Neil opens his play. Todd waits for Neil to relent. He
doesn't.

EXT. SOCCER FIELD - AFTERNOON

Gusts of wind blow across the field. About 50 boys follow
Keating as he leads them to the sidelines.

                    KEATING
          Devotees may argue that one game or
          sport is inherently better than
          another. For me the most important
          thing in all sport is the way other
          human beings can push us to excel.
          Plato, a gifted man like myself,
          said, "Only the contest made me a
          poet, a sophist, an orator." Each
          person take a slip of paper and
          line up single file.

He passes out slips of paper to the curious students.

                    KEATING
          Mr. Meeks, time to inherit the
          earth. Mr. Pitts, rise above your
          name... Conroy, pass the rest of
          these out.

EXT. THE SOCCER FIELD - LATER

The boys form a long line. Ten feet in front of the boy at
the head of the line, a soccer ball rests on the ground.

                    (CONTINUED)

40

CONTINUED:

                         KEATING
          YOU know what to do... now go!

                         FIRST BOY
          "Oh to struggle against great odds,
          To meet enemies undaunted!"

He runs and kicks the ball at the goal, missing. Keating
puts down another ball, then puts a record on a portable
record player. Classical music starts. The second boy,
Knox, steps out.

                         KEATING
          Rhythm, boy! Rhythm is important.

                         SECOND BOY (KNOX)
          "To be entirely alone with them, to
          find out how much one can stand!"

Knox too runs and kicks the ball. Just before he smashes
it with his foot, he angrily yells: "CHET!"

                         THIRD BOY (MEEKS)
          "To look strife, torture, prison,
          popular odium face to face!"

Meeks runs and kicks the ball with great intent. Next,
Charlie steps out.

                         KEATING
          Come on, Charlie. Let it fill your
          soul!

                         CHARLIE
          "To indeed be a God!"

With determination, Charlie kicks the ball through the
goal.

INT. THE DORM HALLWAY - AFTERNOON.

Neil enters, looking exhilarated.

                         NEIL
          I got it. Hey, everybody, I got the
          part! I'm going to play Puck. Hey,
          I'm Puck!

                         VOICE FROM A ROOM
          "Puck" you! Pipe down.

                         CHARLIE AND OTHERS
          All right, Neil. Congratulations!

41

INT. NEIL AND TODD'S ROOM - NIGHT

Neil enters and closes the door. Incredibly excited, he
pulls out an old typewriter and begins to type. Todd
watches.

                    TODD
          Neil, how are you gonna do this?

                    NEIL
          Shsh. That's what I'm taking care
          of. They need a letter of
          permission.

                    TODD
          From you?

                    NEIL
          From my father and Nolan.

                    TODD
          Neil, you're not gonna...

                    NEIL
          Quiet. I have to think.

Neil mumbles lines from the play, giggles to himself, then
keeps typing. Todd shakes his head in disbelief.

INT. KEATING'S CLASSROOM - DAY

Knox stands before class reading the poem he wrote.

                    KNOX
          "I see a sweetness in her smile
          Bright light shines from her eye's
          But life is complete; contentment
          mine Just knowing that she--"

Knox stops. He lowers his paper.

                    KNOX
          I'm sorry, Captain. It's stupid.

Knox walks back to his seat.

                    KEATING
          It's fine, Knox. It's not stupid.
               (to the class)
          What Knox has done demonstrates an
          important point, not only in
          writing poetry, but in every
               (more)

                    (CONTINUED)

42

CONTINUED:

                    KEATING (Cont'd)
          endeavor. That is, deal with the
          important things in life... love,
          beauty, truth, justice.

Keating paces.

                    KEATING
          Mr. Hopkins you were laughing.
          You're next.

Hopkins, a boy who is definitely skeptical of Keating and
all he stands for, walks to the front. He reads from a
slip of paper.

                    HOPKINS
          The cat sat on the mat.

The class laughs. Hopkins walks back to his seat. Keating
walks to him.

                    KEATING
          Congratulations, Mr. Hopkins.
          You're the first person ever to
          receive a negative score on the
          Pritchard scale. I don't mind that
          your poem is about simple things.
          You could write a great poem about
          simple things - music, a flower,
          even a cat - anything with the
          stuff of revelation in it. Just
          don't ever let your poems be
          ordinary. Got it?

Hopkins grudgingly nods. Keating moves on.

                    KEATING
          Okay, who wants to be next? Come
          on. I'll get to everyone
          eventually.

Keating looks around. No one volunteers. Keating grins.

                    KEATING (CONT'D)
          Look at Mr. Anderson. In such
          agony. Step up, Todd, and let's put
          you out of your misery.

All eyes are on Todd. He is dying inside. He stands and
walks slowly to the front of the class like a condemned
man on his way to his execution.

                              (CONTINUED)

43

CONTINUED: (2)

                    KEATING (CONT'D)
          Todd, have you prepared your poem?

Todd shakes his head no.

                    KEATING
          Mr. Anderson believes that
          everything he has inside of him is
          worthless and embarrassing.
          Correct, Todd? Isn't that your
          fear?

Todd nods jerkedly yes.

                    KEATING (CONT'D)
          Then today you will see that what
          is inside of you is worth a great
          deal.

Keating strides to the blackboard. Rapidly, he writes:

"I SOUND MY BARBARIC YAWP OVER THE ROOFTOPS OF THE WORLD."
                    -- Walt Whitman

                    KEATING (CONT'D)
          A yawp, for those who don't know,
          is a loud cry or yell. Todd, I
          would like you to give us a
          demonstration of a barbaric yawp.

                    TODD
               (barely audible)
          A yawp?

                    KEATING
          A barbaric yawp.

                    TODD
          Yawp.

Keating pauses, then suddenly moves fiercely at Todd.

                    KEATING
          Good god, boy, yell!

                    TODD
               (frightened)
          Yawp!

                    KEATING
          Again! Louder!

                    (CONTINUED)

44

CONTINUED: (3)

                    TODD
          YAWP!

                    KEATING
          LOUDER!

                    TODD
          AHHHHHHH!

                    KEATING
          All right! There's a barbarian in
          there after all!

Todd starts to sit. Keating doesn't let him.

                    KEATING
          Hold on. You don't get away that
          easily. Todd, there's a picture of
          Whitman over the door. What does he
          remind you of? Quickly, Anderson,
          don't think about it.

                    TODD
          A madman.

                    KEATING
          A madman. What kind of madman?
          Don't think! Answer.

                    TODD
          A... crazy madman.

                    KEATING
          Use your imagination! First thing
          that pops to your mind, even if
          it's gibberish!

                    TODD
          A... a... sweaty-toothed madman.

                    KEATING
          Now there's the poet speaking!
          Close your eyes. Describe what you
          see. NOW!

                    TODD
          I... I close my eyes. His image
          floats beside me.

                    KEATING
                 (prompting)
          A sweaty-toothed madman...

                         (CONTINUED)

45

CONTINUED: (4)

                     TODD
A sweaty-toothed madman...

                     KEATING
Good...

                     TODD
With a stare that pounds my brain.

                     KEATING
Excellent! Have him act. Give it
rhythm!

                     TODD
His hands reach out and choke me...

                     KEATING
Yes.

                     TODD
All the time he mumbles slowly...

                     KEATING
Mumbles what?

                     TODD
Truth... truth is like a blanket
that always leaves your feet cold.

This brings chuckles from the class. This distracts Todd.

                     KEATING
To hell with them, more about the
blanket!

                     TODD
Stretch it, pull it, it will never
cover any of us.

                     KEATING
Go on!

                     TODD
Kick at it, beat at it, it will
never be enough...

                     KEATING
Don't stop!

                     (CONTINUED)

46

CONTINUED: (5)

> TODD
> (struggling, but getting it
> out)
> From the moment we enter crying to
> the moment we leave dying, It will
> cover just your head as you wail
> and cry and scream!

Todd stands still for a long time. Both he and the
students have felt the magic of what has just taken place.
Neil starts applauding. Others join in. Todd swells and,
for the first time, there is a hint of confidence in him.
The applause stops. Keating walks to Todd.

> KEATING
> Don't you forget this.

EXT. THE SOCCER FIELD - DAY

A soccer ball careens off a kicking foot. Beethoven's
Ninth Symphony, fourth movement, "Ode To Joy," blares
forth. Keating stands on the sidelines beside his portable
record player, watching the boys play soccer, waving his
arms like an orchestra conductor. In front of Keating the
boys play soccer to this spectacular music. They run,
kick, pass, fall, block, head, dribble, fake -- all to the
overpowering chorus of one of the most inspirational
pieces of music ever written.

EXT. WOODS, DAY.

Neil crosses the dam on the creek, heading towards the
cave. He carries a battered lampshade.

EXT. DEAD POETS CAVE - AFTERNOON

Neil enters the cave.

INT. DEAD POETS CAVE - AFTERNOON

Neil hurries in carrying the lampshade. The other
"pledges" of the Dead Poets Society are assembled around
Charlie who sits silently cross-legged before them. His
eyes are closed and, in one hand, he holds an old
saxophone.

> NEIL
> Look at this.

(CONTINUED)

47

CONTINUED:

                    MEEKS
          What is it?

                    PITTS
          Duh uh. It's a lampshade, Meeks.

Neil takes off the lampshade, pulls out the cord,
revealing a small painted statue.

                    NEIL
          It's the god of the cave.

                    MEEKS
          Duh uh, Pitts!

The statue has a stake sticking out of its head with a
candle stuck in it. Neil plants the statue in ground and
lights the candle. It illuminates a red and blue drummer
boy, face pitted from exposure, yet noble in its visage.
Todd playfully puts the lampshade on his own head.
Charlie, who hasn't moved, clears his throat. All turn to
him and settle in.

                    CHARLIE
          Gentlemen, "Poetrusic" by Charles
          Dalton.

He blows scattered notes on the saxophone. Random,
blaring, they sound like bad John Cage. Suddenly Charlie
stops.

                    CHARLIE (CONT'D)
              (trance-like, run-on delivery)
          Laughing, crying, tumbling,
          mumbling, gotta do more. Gotta be
          more...

He plays more notes on the sax, then:

                    CHARLIE (CONT'D)
              (more rapid than before)
          Chaos screaming, chaos dreaming,
          crying, flying, gotta be more!!
          Gotta be more!!

Charlie plays a simple but absolutely gorgeous melody. The
skeptical looks on the faces of the boys disappear. As
Charlie gets lost in the music, so do the others. The
melody ends with a long, beautiful, haunting note.

                    NEIL
          Charlie, that was great! Where did
          you learn to play like that?

                              (CONTINUED)

48

CONTINUED: (2)

                    CHARLIE
          My parents made me take clarinet
          for years.

                    CAMERON
          I love the clarinet.

                    CHARLIE
          I hated it.
                    (pauses)
          The sax is more sonorous.

                    PITTS
          Whoa. A big word.

Knox stands. He backs away, full of torment and
frustration.

                    KNOX
          God, I can't take it anymore! If I
          don't have Chris, I'll kill myself.

                    CHARLIE
          Knox, you gotta calm down.

                    KNOX
          No, I've been calm all my life! If
          I don't do something, it's gonna
          kill me.

                    NEIL
          Where are you going?

                    KNOX
          I'm calling her!

INT. THE DORM PHONE ROOM - LATER

All of the boys stand around. Knox picks up the phone,
boldly dials some numbers, then waits.

                    CHRIS (O.S.)
          Hello?

Knox hears Chris' voice. He hangs up the phone.

                    KNOX
          She's gonna hate me! The Danburrys
          will hate me. My parents will kill
          me!

                    (CONTINUED)

49

CONTINUED:

He looks at the faces of the others. No one says a word.

> KNOX (CONT'D)
> All right, goddamn it, you're
> right! 'Carpe diem' even if it
> kills me.

He picks up the phone and dials again.

> CHRIS (O.S.)
> Hello?

> KNOX
> Hello Chris, this is Knox
> Overstreet.

> CHRIS (O.S.)
> Knox... Oh yes, Knox. I'm glad you
> called.

> KNOX
> You are?
>   (excitedly, to his friends)
> She's glad I called!

> CHRIS (O.S.)
> I wanted to call you but I didn't
> have the number. Chet's parents are
> going out of town this weekend so
> Chet's having a party. Would you
> like to come?

> KNOX
> Well, sure!

> CHRIS (O.S.)
> Chet's parents don't know about it
> so please keep it quiet. But you
> can bring someone if you like.

> KNOX
> I'll be there. The Danburrys.
> Friday night. Thank you, Chris.

He hangs up the phone. He is thunderstruck. He lets out a
yelp.

> KNOX (CONT'D)
> Can you believe it? She was gonna
> call me! She invited me to a party!

(CONTINUED)

50

CONTINUED: (2)

                    CHARLIE
          At Chet Danburry's house.

                    KNOX
          Yeah.

                    CHARLIE
          Well?

                    KNOX
          So?

                    CHARLIE
          So you really think she means
          you're going with her?

                    KNOX
          Well hell no, Charlie, but that's
          not the point. That's not the point
          at all!

                    CHARLIE
          What is the point?

                    KNOX
          The point is... she was thinking
          about me!

                    CHARLIE
          Ah.

                    KNOX
          I've only met her once and already
          she's thinking about me. Damn it,
          it's gonna happen! I feel it. She's
          going to be mine!

He exits the phone room, his head in a cloud. The others
look at each other, not sure what to think.

EXT. THE WELTON DORMS - NIGHT

Neil starts into the dorm. He spots a figure sitting
motionless on a wall.

                    NEIL
          Todd?

Neil walks over to get a better look. It is Todd, sitting
in the dark without a coat.

                                        (CONTINUED)

51

CONTINUED:

                    NEIL
          What's going on?

                    TODD
          It's my birthday.

                    NEIL
          It is? Happy Birthday. What'd you
          get?

Todd points to a box. Neil looks. In the box seems to be
the monogrammed desk set that we've seen on Todd's desk.

                    NEIL
          Isn't this your desk set?

                    TODD
          They gave me the exact same thing
          as last year.

                    NEIL
          Oh.

                    TODD
          Oh.

Long pause.

                    NEIL
          Well, maybe they thought you'd need
          another one. Maybe they thought...

                    TODD
          Maybe they don't think at all
          unless it's about my brother.
               (pause; looks at the desk set)
          The stupid thing is, I didn't even
          like the first one.

He looks away.

                    NEIL
          Look, Todd, you're obviously
          under-estimating the value of this
          desk set.

                    TODD
          What?

                    NEIL
          I mean who would want a football or
          a baseball bat -

                              (CONTINUED)

52

CONTINUED: (2)

> TODD
> Or a <u>car</u>.

> NEIL
> Or a car - when they could get a
> desk set as wonderful as this one!
> If I were going to give anybody a
> desk set - twice - it would
> definitely be this. In fact, I
> think this desk set is rather -
> aerodynamic.

> TODD
> What?

> NEIL
> This desk set wants... to fly.

Todd suddenly realizes what Neil is getting at. He takes
the desk set and grips it.

> NEIL
> The world's first unmanned flying
> desk set.

Todd flings the desk set. It comes to pieces in the air.
Neil and Todd laugh.

> NEIL
> Oh well, I wouldn't worry if I were
> you. You'll get another one next
> year.

Todd laughs.

EXT. A WELTON BRICK COURTYARD - DAY

The class stands in the courtyard expectantly. Another
Keating stunt? Keating addresses them.

> KEATING
> Misters Pitts, Cameron, Overstreet,
> on the count of four, begin walking
> together around the courtyard.
> Nothing to think about. No grade
> here. One, two, three, go.

The boys begin walking. They go down one side of the
courtyard, across the back, up the other side, then across
the front.

(CONTINUED)

53

CONTINUED:

                    KEATING (CONT'D)
          That's the way.

As the boys walk around the courtyard again, they begin to
walk together in step. Soon it becomes like a march,
producing a one-two-three-four cadence. Keating begins to
clap.

                    KEATING (CONT'D)
          There it is... Hear it?
               (clapping louder in time)
          One two, one two, one two, one
          two...
               (rhythmically:)
          We're all having fun, In Mr.
          Keating's class...

ANGLE FROM ABOVE

The marching boys get into it. The class joins in
clapping. Soon the four boys are marching vigorously to
the rhythmic clapping of the entire class. Keating joins
in marching with them.

                    KEATING
          One two three four left right halt!

NEW ANGLE

Inside his second-story office, Nolan is looking out his
window at the marching boys below.

ANGLE ON KEATING

                    KEATING (CONT'D)
          Now you may have noticed how at the
          beginning Misters Overstreet and
          Pitts seemed to have a different
          stride than the others - Pitts with
          his long lurches, Cameron
          tentative, Overstreet drawn by a
          greater force ....
               (Keating imitates the boys'
               walks)
          Now this experiment was not to
          single out Pitts or Overstreet.
          What it demonstrates is how
          difficult it is for any of us to
          listen to our own voice or maintain
          our own beliefs in the presence of
          others.
                    (more)

                    (CONTINUED)

54

CONTINUED: (2)

                    KEATING (Cont'd)
          And if any of you think you would
          have marched differently, then ask
          yourself why you were clapping.
          Lads, there is a great need in all
          of us to be accepted, but you must
          trust what is unique or different
          about yourself even if its odd or
          unpopular. As Frost said, "Two
          roads diverged in a wood, and I...
          I took the one less traveled by,
          And that has made all the
          difference." Gentlemen, I'd like
          you to take a few moments to
          practice your own walk. No grades
          here. The courtyard is yours.

The boys begin walking around the courtyard, some
thinking, some clowning. Charlie stands without walking.

                    KEATING
          Would you care to join in, Mr.
          Daulton?

                    CHARLIE
          Exercising the right not to walk,
          sir.

                    KEATING
          Thank you Mr. Daulton, you just
          illustrated the point.

ANGLE ON NOLAN IN HIS OFFICE

Nolan moves away from the window.

INT. THE DEAD POETS CAVE - NIGHT
Todd, Neil, Cameron, Pitts, and Meeks sit around.

                    MEEKS
          Where's Knox?

                    PITTS
          Getting ready for that party.

                    CAMERON
          What about Charlie? He's the one
          who insisted on this meeting.

                    (CONTINUED)

CONTINUED:

                    NEIL
          "I went to the woods because I
          wanted to live deliberately. To...

In the woods there is a noise... the sound of girls'
laughter.

                    GIRL'S VOICE
          I can't see a thing.

                    CHARLIE'S VOICE
          It's just over here.

Charlie and TWO GIRLS enter the cave. One is pretty, the
other is plain. The girls are about 20, blonde, not the
type to be seriously interested in Charlie or the other
boys. They're just here for a good time.

                    CHARLIE
          Hey guys, meet Gloria and...

                    PLAIN GIRL (TINA)
          Tina.

                    CHARLIE
          Tina and Gloria, this is the pledge
          class of the Dead Poets Society.

                    GLORIA
          It's such a strange name! Won't you
          tell us what it means?

                    CHARLIE
          I told you, that's a secret.

                    GLORIA
          Isn't he precious?

Gloria gives Charlie an affectionate hug. The other
members of the club are flabbergasted. These girls are
wild, exotic creatures, the kind whose unashamed love of
men causes young boys' hearts to come to rest in young
boys' throats.

                    CHARLIE
          Guys, I have an announcement. In
          keeping with the spirit of
          passionate experimentation of the
          Dead Poets, I'm giving up the name
          Charles Dalton. From now on, call
          me "Nuwanda."

The girls giggle.

                              (CONTINUED)

56

CONTINUED: (2)

                   TINA
      I can't call you Charlie anymore?
        (puts her arm around Charlie)
      What's Numama mean, honey?

                 CHARLIE
      It's Nuwanda, and I made it up.

INT. THE DANBURRY HOUSE - NIGHT.

Knox enters. Rock music is playing on the Hi-Fi. On the
entrance hall couch is a couple, making out like crazy. Up
and down the stairs are other couples doing the same. Knox
stands there, not knowing what to do. Momentarily, Chris
walks through, her hair an uncombed mess.

                 KNOX
      Chris!

Chris turns and sees Knox.

                 CHRIS
      Oh, hi. I'm glad you made it. Did
      you bring anybody?

                 KNOX
      No.

                 CHRIS
      Ginny Danburry's here. Look for
      her.

                 KNOX
      But Chris...

                 CHRIS
      I gotta find Chet. Make yourself at
      home.

She exits. Knox watches her. He slumps in dejection.

INT. THE DANBURRY PARTY - NIGHT

Knox, looking suicidal, wanders through the crowded party.
Kids stand talking. A couple in the corner is involved in
a long kiss. His hand keeps wandering to her knee and her
hand keeps pushing his away, yet the kiss never breaks.
Knox watches this then glances across the room and spots:

                (CONTINUED)

57

CONTINUED:

Chris dancing with Chet. Knox frowns and moves to the beer keg in the kitchen. At the sink a guy stands making bourbon and Cokes. The guy eyes Knox.

                    GUY
          You Mutt Sanders' brother?

Knox shakes his head no.

                    GUY (CONT'D)
          Bubba...

BUBBA is a big, drunk jock leaning on the refrigerator.

                    GUY (CONT'D)
          This guy look like Mutt Sanders?

                    BUBBA
          You his brother?

                    KNOX
          No relation. Never heard of him.
          Sorry.

                    BUBBA
          Say Steve, where's your manners?
          Here's Mutt's brother and you don't
          offer him a drink? Want some
          whiskey?

                    KNOX
          Actually I don't...

Steve puts a glass in Knox's hand and fills it with whiskey. Bubba clinks the glass with him.

                    BUBBA
          To Mutt.

                    STEVE
          To Mutt.

                    KNOX
          To... Mutt.

Bubba and Steve drain their glasses. Knox follows their lead, then bursts into a coughing fit. Steve pours everyone more whiskey.

                    BUBBA
          So what the hell's Mutt been up to?

                              (CONTINUED)

58

CONTINUED: (2)

                    KNOX
               (coughing fitfully)
          Actually... I don't really... know
          Mutt.

                    BUBBA
               (toasting)
          To the mighty Mutt.

                    STEVE
          To mighty Mutt.

                    KNOX
          Mighty... Mutt...

They drain their glasses again. Knox continues coughing.

                    BUBBA
          Well, I'd better find Patsy.
               (slaps Knox on the back)
          Say hello to Mutt for me.

                    KNOX
          Will do.

Coughing, Knox downs more whiskey.

INT. THE CAVE - NIGHT

Tina takes out a pint of bourbon and offers some to Neil.
He takes it and sips. He obviously hasn't had much whiskey
in his life but he tries to act like he has. He hands it
back.

                    TINA (CONT'D)
          Go ahead, pass it around.

Neil does. It goes from boy to boy. Each boy tries to act
like he likes the terrible bitterness he tastes.

                    CHARLIE
          Say are we gonna have a meeting or
          what?

                    GLORIA
          Yeah. How do we know if we want to
          join if you don't have a meeting?

                         (CONTINUED)

59

CONTINUED:

                    NEIL
               (casts a surprised look at
               Charlie)
          Join?

Charlie ignores this. He turns to Tina.

                    CHARLIE
          "Shall I compare thee to a summer's
          day? Thou art more lovely and more
          temperate..."

In his recital, Charlie has aimed these words directly at
Tina. She melts into warm goo.

                    TINA
          Oh, that's so sweet!

Tina hugs Charlie. The other boys look at each other,
trying unsuccessfully to hide their incredible jealousy.

                    CHARLIE
          I wrote that for you.

                    TINA
          You did?!

                    CHARLIE
          I'll write one for you too, Gloria.
               (closes his eyes then)
          "She walks in beauty like the
          night..."

Charlie's eyes open. He has forgotten the words to this
poem.

                    CHARLIE (CONT'D)
          "She walks in beauty like the
          night..."

Charlie turns his back, opens a book, and reads quickly to
himself. He closes it, puts the book down, and turns back
to Gloria.

                    CHARLIE (CONT'D)
          "Of cloudless climes and starry
          skies; All that's best of dark and
          bright Meet in her aspect and her
          eyes."

Gloria squeals with delight.

                         (CONTINUED)

60

CONTINUED: (2)

                        GLORIA
              That's so wonderful?!

The other boys are absolutely appalled, but desperately
jealous that Charlie is getting away with this. Gloria
hugs Charlie.

                        CHARLIE
              There's plenty more where that came
              from.

INT. THE DANBURRY LIVING ROOM - NIGHT

Music is playing loudly. Every light in the room is out.
The only illumination is moonlight through the windows.
Only after our eyes get adjusted to the dark can we see
that the room is filled with couples making out.

Knox, carrying another drink and looking tipsy, enters. He
walks a bit, then trips over a couple on the floor.

                        ANGRY GUY'S VOICE
              Hey!

                        KNOX
              Sorry.

Knox falls onto the sofa. To his left sit a couple making
out heavily. Their breathing is like that of some giant
beast. Knox tries to get up but the couple he tripped over
has now rolled against his shins, pinning him. Knox tries
to get comfortable in his little spot on the sofa.

The music stops. The room sounds like an artificial
respiration ward. Knox glances to his left then glances
again. Lying on the couch, napping, is Chris. Knox looks
around. Chet is across the room, downing drinks with Bubba
and Steve. Knox tries but he can't keep his eyes off
Chris.

                        KNOX
              Oh my God help me.

Chris shifts her position to get comfortable. Her head is
practically in Knox' lap. Knox looks around and sees that
he is not being watched. He realizes that this might be
his only chance.

                        KNOX (CONT'D)
                   (to himself)
              Carpe diem... Carpe Diem!

                        (CONTINUED)

61

CONTINUED:

As though his hand were being drawn by a magnet too
powerful to resist, Knox' hand reaches out and begins to
ever so lightly stroke the nape of Chris' neck and her
hair. Chris smiles in her sleep. Knox moves his hand up
and down her, sensuously. He closes his eyes; he has found
his dream and he is touching her.

                    CHRIS
          Mmm.

Knox pulls his hand away.

                         CHRIS
                    (still asleep)
          Don't stop.

Knox puts his hand back on Chris' neck. Again he starts
stroking her, ever so delicately. He downs some more
whiskey then musters his courage. He leans over and kisses
her.

ACROSS THE ROOM

Bubba is downing drinks with Steve and Chet. He thinks he
sees something then squints to make sure it's for real.

                         BUBBA
          Chet...Chet, would you look!

Knox hears Bubba and freezes.

                         BUBBA
          Mutt Sanders brother is feelin up
          your girl!

Chet sees what Bubba is talking about and moves across the
room.

                         CHET
          What are you doing?!

                         KNOX
          Now, Chet, I know this looks bad
          but I can explain...

                         CHET
          Why you...

Chet smashes Knox in the face with his fist. He grabs Knox
by the shirt, throws him to the floor, and jumps on him.
He begins swinging at Knox's face which Knox is doing his
best to protect.

                         (CONTINUED)

62

CONTINUED: (2)

>   CHET (CONT'D)
>   You little jerk!
>
>   CHRIS
>   (beginning to feel sorry for
>   Knox)
>   Chet, you're hurting him.

Chet's fists hit Knox over and over.

>   CHRIS (CONT'D)
>   Chet, stop!

She pushes Chet off. Knox rolls over, holding his face.
Chet stands over Knox, who is holding his bloody nose and
bruised face.

>   KNOX
>   I'm sorry, Chris. I'm sorry!
>
>   CHET
>   You want some more? Huh?! Chris,
>   get away from him.

He moves at Knox again, but Chris and some others hold him
back.

>   KNOX
>   Chris, I'm sorry!
>
>   CHET
>   Next time I see you, you're dead!

INT. THE CAVE, NIGHT.

There is an awkward silence. Charlie would clearly like to
be alone with Gloria but there is no way to engineer that.
Meeks tries to strike up conversation with the girls.

>   MEEKS
>   Me and Pitts are working on a hi-fi
>   system. It shouldn't be that hard
>   to put together.

Another awkward pause.

>   PITTS
>   I might be going to Yale. Then
>   again, I might not.

                         (CONTINUED)

63

CONTINUED:

                    GLORIA
          Don't you guys miss having girls
          here?

                    MEEKS AND PITTS
               (too quickly)
          Yeah!

                    CHARLIE
          It drives us crazy. That's part of
          what this club is about. In fact,
          I'd like to announce that I've
          published an article in the school
          paper, in the name of the Dead
          Poets Society, demanding girls be
          admitted to Welton, so we can all
          stop beating off.

                    NEIL
          You what?! How did you do that?

                    CHARLIE
          I'm one of the proofers. I slipped
          the article in.

                    PITTS
          Oh god, it's over now!

                    CHARLIE
          Why? Nobody knows who we are.

                    CAMERON
          Don't you think they'll figure out
          who did it?! Don't you know they'll
          come to you and demand to know what
          the Dead Poets Society is? Charlie,
          you had no right to do something
          like that!

                    CHARLIE
          It's Nuwanda, Cameron.

                    GLORIA
               (putting her arm around
                Charlie)
          That's right, it's Nuwanda.

                    CHARLIE
          And are we just playing around out
          here or do we mean what we say? If
          all we do is come and read a bunch
          of poems to each other, what the
          hell are we doing?

                              (CONTINUED)

64

CONTINUED: (2)

                    NEIL
          You still shouldn't have done it.
          You don't speak for the club.

                    CHARLIE
          Hey, would you not worry about your
          precious little necks? If they
          catch me, I'll tell them I made it
          up.

INT. WELTON ACADEMY CHAPEL - DAY

There is a buzz in the student body as they move to the
pews. Mr. Nolan enters, carrying a school newspaper. All
stand. Nolan strides to the podium and motions for
everyone to sit. All obey.

                    NOLAN
          In this week's issue of Welton
          Honor, there appeared an
          unauthorized and profane article
          about the need for girls at Welton.
          Rather than spend my valuable time
          ferreting out the guilty parties --
          and let me assure you I -- will
          find them -- I am asking any and
          all students who know anything
          about this article to make
          themselves known here and now.
          Whoever the guilty persons are,
          this is your only chance to avoid
          expulsion from this school.

Suddenly, somewhere in the room, there is the sound of a
TELEPHONE RINGING. Charlie briskly lifts the briefcase
into his lap and opens it. Inside the briefcase is a
ringing telephone. Everyone in assembly is astounded. No
one has ever done something this outrageous here. Charlie,
undaunted, seemingly serious, answers the phone.

                    CHARLIE (INTO PHONE)
                 (for all to hear)
          Welton Academy, hello? Yes, he is,
          just a moment. Mr. Nolan, it's for
          you.

                    NOLAN
          What?!

Charlie holds the receiver out to Nolan.

                    (CONTINUED)

65

CONTINUED:

                    CHARLIE (INTO PHONE)
          It's God. He says we should have
          girls at Welton.

There is a blast of laughter from the students.

INT. NOLAN'S OFFICE - DAY

Charlie stands in the middle of the room. Nolan paces
furiously.

                    NOLAN
          Wipe that smirk off your face. Who
          else was involved in this?

                    CHARLIE
          No one, sir. It was just me. I did
          the proofing so I inserted my
          article in place of Rob Crane's.

                    NOLAN
          Mr. Dalton, if you think you're the
          first to try to get thrown out of
          this school, think again. Others
          have had similar notions and they
          have failed just as surely as you
          will fail. Assume the position.

Charlie flips up his coat and bends over. Nolan produces a
paddle. The paddle has holes drilled in it to speed its
progress. Nolan takes off his jacket and moves behind
Charlie.

                    NOLAN
          Count aloud, Mr. Dalton.

He slams the paddle into Charlie's buttocks.

                    CHARLIE
          One...

Nolan swings the paddle again. This time he gets more
power into it. Charlie winces.

                    CHARLIE (CONT'D)
          Two...

Nolan delivers and Charlie counts. By the fourth lick, the
pain is so intense that Charlie is barely audible. Nolan
pauses.

                    (CONTINUED)

66

CONTINUED:

                         NOLAN
          What is this "Dead Poets Society"?
          I want names.

INT. THE JUNIOR DORM - AFTERNOON

The boys are milling in their rooms, waiting for Charlie's
return. Someone sees him coming.

Charlie enters, moving slowly, trying not to show his
pain. As he walks toward his room, Neil, Todd, Knox
(bruised face), Pitts, and Meeks approach him.

                         NEIL
          What happened? Were you kicked out?

                         CHARLIE
              (not looking at anyone)
          No.

                         NEIL
          What happened?

                         CHARLIE
          I'm supposed to turn everybody in,
          apologize to the school, and all
          will be forgiven.

Charlie heads into his room. The others look at each
other.

                         NEIL
          What are you going to do?...
          Charlie?

                         CHARLIE
          Damn it, Neil, the name is Nuwanda.

Charlie gives the boys a pregnant look, then goes into his
room and closes his door. Smiles of admiration cross the
boys' faces. Charlie has not been broken.

INT. WELTON CLASSROOM BUILDING- AFTERNOON

Mr. Nolan walks down the corridor. He stops at the door to
Keating's classroom, then enters.

INT. KEATING'S CLASSROOM - DAY

Keating and McAllister are talking. Nolan enters.
                         (CONTINUED)

67

CONTINUED:

                    NOLAN
          Mr. Keating, may we have a word?

                    McALLISTER
          Excuse me.

McAllister leaves. Nolan pauses and looks around.

                    NOLAN
          This was my first classroom, John,
          did you know that?
                    (looks at Keating's desk)
          My first desk.

                    KEATING
          I didn't know you taught.

                    NOLAN
          English. Way before your time. It
          was hard giving it up, I'll tell
          you.
                    (pause)
          I'm hearing rumors, John, of some
          unorthodox teaching methods in your
          classroom. I'm not saying they have
          anything to do with the Dalton
          boy's outburst, but I don't think I
          have to warn you that boys his age
          are very impressionable.

                    KEATING
          Your reprimand made quite an
          impression, I'm sure.

                    NOLAN
                    (letting this pass)
          What was going on in the courtyard
          the other day?

                    KEATING
          Courtyard?

                    NOLAN
          Boys marching. Clapping in
          unison...

                    KEATING
          Oh that. That was an exercise to
          prove a point. Dangers of
          conformity.

                         (CONTINUED)

68

CONTINUED: (2)

                    NOLAN
          John, the curriculum here is set.
          It's proven. It works. If you
          question it, what's to prevent them
          from doing the same?

                    KEATING
          I always thought education was
          learning to think for yourself.

                    NOLAN
               (almost laughs)
          At these boys' age? Not on your
          life! Tradition, John. Discipline.
               (pats Keating on the shoulder)
          Prepare them for college, and the
          rest will take care of itself.

Mr. Nolan smiles and leaves. Keating stands, thinking.

INT. THE JUNIOR CLASS DORM - NIGHT

Boys are crowded around Charlie who is telling the story
of his paddling. Keating enters.

                    CHARLIE
               (surprised)
          Mr. Keating!

                    KEATING
          That was a ridiculous stunt, Mr.
          Dalton.

                    CHARLIE
          You're siding with Mr. Nolan?! What
          about carpe diem and sucking all
          the marrow out of life and all
          that?

                    KEATING
          Sucking out the marrow doesn't mean
          getting the bone stuck in your
          throat. There is a place for daring
          and a place for caution and a wise
          man understands which is called
          for.

                    CHARLIE
          But I thought...

                              (CONTINUED)

69

CONTINUED:

                    KEATING
          Getting expelled from this school
          is not an act of wisdom. It's far
          from perfect but there are still
          opportunities to be had here.

                    CHARLIE
          Yeah? Like what?

                    KEATING
          Like, if nothing else, the
          opportunity to attend my classes,
          understand?

                    CHARLIE (smiling)
          Yes sir.

                    KEATING
          So keep your head about you --the
          lot of you.

                    NEIL, TODD, PITTS, MEEKS, CAMERON, KNOX
          Yes sir.

Keating gives them a slight smile, then turns to leave.

                    KEATING
          Phone call from god...

He stops at the door.

                    KEATING
          If it had been collect, that would
          have been daring.

EXT. THE HENLEY HALL AUDITORIUM - DAY

Neil parks his bicycle and enters the auditorium.

INT. THE AUDITORIUM STAGE - LATER

High school actors are on stage rehearsing Shakespeare's
"A Midsummer Night's Dream." Neil enters then pauses in
the back of the auditorium to watch. As the takes in the
costumes, the actors, the director giving directions, a
smile of joy crosses his face. This is where he has longed
to be.

70

INT. DORM HALLWAY - DUSK

Neil jesters his way down the hall, passing other students
on their way to dinner.

                    NEIL
          Save some for me, guys.
              (to himself)
          Alas fairy, here comes Oberon...

INT. TODD AND NEIL'S DORM ROOM - DUSK

Neil enters in a whirlwind of excitement. He turns and
sees his father, sitting at his desk.

                    NEIL
          Father!

                    MR. PERRY
          Neil, you are going to quit this
          ridiculous play immediately.

                    NEIL
          Father, I--

Mr. Perry jumps to his feet.
                    MR. PERRY
          Don't you dare talk back to me!!
          It's bad enough that you've wasted
          your time with this absurd acting
          business. But you deliberately
          deceived me!
              (paces furiously)
          How did you expect to get away with
          this? Answer me! Who put you up to
          it? This new man, this Keating?

                    NEIL
          Nobody. I thought I'd surprise you.
          I've got all A's and...

                    MR. PERRY
          Did you really think I wouldn't
          find out? "My niece is in a play
          with your son," Mrs. Marks says.
          "You must be mistaken," I say. "My
          son isn't in a play." You made a
          liar out of me, Neil! Now you will
          go tomorrow and tell them you are
          quitting.

                    (CONTINUED)

71

CONTINUED:

                        NEIL
          Father, I have the main part. The
          performance is tomorrow night.
          Father, please...

                      MR. PERRY
          I don't care if the world is coming
          to an end tomorrow night, you are
          through with that play. Is that
          clear? Is that clear!

                      NEIL
          Yes sir.

Mr. Perry stops. He stares hard at his son.

                      MR. PERRY
          I've made great sacrifices to get
          you here, Neil. You will not let me
          down.

He turns and exits. Neil stands there for a long time.

                      NEIL
          Yes sir.

Neil's father leaves. Neil is left alone, tears streaming
down his face.

EXT. KEATING'S ROOM - EVENING

Keating's quarters cramped. Keating sits at his desk,
picture of a girl before him, writing her a letter. There
is a knock at the door.

                      KEATING
          It's open.

Neil opens the door and enters. Keating sees him and
stands.

                      KEATING
          Well hello. Come in. Can I offer
          you some tea?

                      NEIL
          Sure. Thanks.

Keating pours some tea from a nearby teapot. Neil looks
around.

                  (CONTINUED)

72

CONTINUED:

                    NEIL
          Gosh, they don't give you much room
          around here, do they?

                    KEATING
               (wryly)
          Part of the monastic oath. They
          don't want worldly things
          distracting me from my teaching.

                    NEIL
          Why do you do put up with it?

                    KEATING
          Because I love teaching. Besides,
          this place needs at least one
          teacher like me.
               (smiles at his joke, then:)
          Did you come here to talk about my
          teaching?

                    NEIL
          My father is making me quit the
          play I'm in at Henley Hall. When I
          think about carpe diem and all
          that, I feel like I'm in prison!
          Acting is everything to me, Mr.
          Keating. It's what I want to do. Of
          course, I can see my father's
          point. We're not a rich family like
          Charlie's. But he's planned the
          rest of my life for me and he's
          never even asked me what I want.

                    KEATING
          Have you told your father what you
          just told me? About your passion
          for acting?

                    NEIL
          Are you kidding? He'd kill me!

                    KEATING
          Then you're playing a part for him
          too, aren't you? The part of the
          dutiful son.

Keating watches Neil who looks uncomfortable.

                         (CONTINUED)

73

CONTINUED: (2)

>   KEATING (CONT'D)
>   Neil, I know this seems impossible
>   but you have to talk to your father
>   and let him know who you really
>   are.

>   NEIL
>   But I know what he'll say. He'll
>   say that acting is just a whim and
>   that it's frivolous and that I
>   should forget about it. He'll tell
>   me how they're counting on me and
>   to put it out of my mind "for my
>   own good."

>   KEATING
>   Well, if it's more than a whim,
>   prove it to him. Show him with your
>   passion and commitment that it's
>   what you really want to do. If that
>   doesn't work, at least by then
>   you'll be eighteen and able to do
>   what you want.

>   NEIL
>   Eighteen! What about the play? The
>   performance is tomorrow night.

>   KEATING
>   Then you'll have to talk to him
>   before tomorrow night.

>   NEIL
>   Isn't there an easier way?

>   KEATING
>   No. Not if you're going to stay
>   true to yourself.

Neil sits there for a long time.

>   NEIL
>   God. I'm trapped.

>   KEATING
>   No, you're not. Talk to your
>   father.

EXT. THE WELTON GROUNDS - EARLY MORNING

The dawn rises over the frozen Welton campus. Snow covers
the ground. The school bagpiper stands, playing a haunting
melody.

74

EXT. THE JUNIOR DORMITORY - SAME

Knox comes out of the dorm building, bundled against the
freezing weather. He hurries onto his bike and speeds
away.

INT. THE HALLWAYS OF RIDGEWAY HIGH - MORNING

Students of both sexes move through the hallways of this
public school. Students are at their lockers, putting up
their coats and getting out their books. Knox runs
through, frantically looking around. He hurries down one
hallway, stops and asks a student something, then runs up
a flight of stairs.

INT. ANOTHER RIDGEWAY HIGH HALLWAY - SAME

Chris stands in front of her locker, chatting with a
couple of girlfriends, taking out some books. Knox spots
her and approaches.

                    KNOX
          Chris!

                    CHRIS
          Knox! What are you doing here?

She pulls Knox away from her girlfriends.

                    KNOX
          I came to apologize for the other
          night. I brought you these and a
          poem I wrote.

He holds out some flowers and the poem. Chris sees them
but doesn't take them.

                    CHRIS
          If Chet sees you, he'll kill you,
          don't you know that?

                    KNOX
          I don't care. I love you, Chris.
          Please accept these.

                    CHRIS
          Knox, you're crazy.

A bell rings. People clear the halls.

                    KNOX
          Please. I acted like a jerk and I
          know it. Please?

                    (CONTINUED)

75

CONTINUED:

She looks at the flowers as if she's thinking about
accepting them.

                    CHRIS
          No! And stop bugging me.

She walks into the classroom and closes the door. The
hallway clears. Knox stands holding his flowers and his
poem. There is a moment's hesitation, then he opens the
door and walks into the classroom.

INT. CHRIS' CLASSROOM - SAME

Class hasn't started but students are taking their seats.
The teacher leans over a student's desk, helping her with
her homework. Knox enters and walks to Chris' desk.

                    CHRIS
          Knox, I don't believe this.

                    KNOX
          All I'm asking you to do is listen.
               (he opens his poem and reads)
          "The heavens made a girl named
          Chris, With hair and skin of gold
          To touch her would be paradise To
          kiss her... glory untold."

Chris turns red with embarrassment. Her friends restrain
giggles. Knox continues reading.

INT. THE WELTON KITCHEN - DAY

Knox enters cold but triumphant. He grabs a roll as he
passes through.

INT. A HALLWAY OUTSIDE THE CLASSROOM, SAME.

Students move through the corridor. Knox hurriedly grabs
his books and joins his friends who are on their way to
another class.

                    CHARLIE
          How'd it go? Did you read it to
          her?

                    KNOX
          Yep.

                    (CONTINUED)

76

CONTINUED:

                    PITTS
          All right! What'd she say?

                    KNOX
          I don't know.

                    CHARLIE
          What do you mean you don't know?

They head off down the hall.

                    CHARLIE
          What do you mean you don't know?!

INT. KEATING'S ENGLISH CLASSROOM - DAY

Most of the class has exited Keating's class. Neil is at
his desk, closing up his books. Keating approaches him.

                    KEATING
          Did you talk to your father?

                    NEIL
               (lying)
          Yeah.

                    KEATING
          Really? Did you tell him what you
          told me? Did you let him see your
          passion for acting?

                    NEIL
          Yeah. He didn't like it one bit but
          at least he's letting me stay in
          the play. Of course, he won't be
          able to come. He'll be in Chicago
          on business. But I think he's gonna
          let me stay with acting. As long as
          I keep up my grades.
               (Neil collects his books)
          Thanks, Mr. Keating.

Neil walks out of the classroom. Keating watches him.

INT. THE DORM BATHROOM, NIGHT.

Todd, Knox, Cameron, Pitts, and Meeks all wear coats and
ties. They mill in front of the mirror, preening.

                    (CONTINUED)

77

CONTINUED:

                  MEEKS
Where's Nuwanda? We're gonna miss
Neil's entrance.

                  PITTS
He said something about getting red
before he left.

                  CAMERON
What does that mean?

                  PITTS
You know Charlie.

Charlie enters.

                  MEEKS
What's this getting red?

Charlie opens his shirt, revealing that he has painted a
red lightning bolt on his chest. The boys laugh.

                  TODD
What's it for?

                  CHARLIE
It's an Indian warrior symbol for
virility. Makes me feel potent.
Like I can drive girls crazy.

                  PITTS
But what if they see it, Nuwanda?

                  CHARLIE
                (winks)
So much the better.

The others shoot each other looks, confirming their mutual
suspicion that Charlie has finally lost his marbles. As
they head out into the lobby, they see Chris, who is
entering.

                  KNOX
Chris!

                  CHRIS
Knox, why are you doing this to me?

                  KNOX
                (looking around)
You can't be in here.

                 (CONTINUED)

78

CONTINUED: (2)

Down the hall appears Mr. Keating, ready to go.

                    KEATING
          Come on, fellows.

The others head towards Keating. Knox leads Chris out.

                    KNOX
               (to his friends)
          I'll be right there.

EXT. THE DORM BUILDING - NIGHT

It is snowing. Knox ushers Chris out of the building.

                    KNOX
          If they catch you here, we'll both
          be in big trouble.

                    CHRIS
          Oh, but it's fine for you to come
          barging into my school and make a
          complete fool out of me?

                    KNOX
          I didn't mean to make a fool of
          you.

                    CHRIS
          Well, you did! Chet found out and
          it was everything I could do to
          keep him from coming here and
          killing you. You have to stop this
          stuff, Knox.

                    KNOX
          But I love you.

                    CHRIS
          You say that over and over but you
          don't even know me!

In the distance, Keating and the others get into the
school woody. The horn toots for Knox.

                    KNOX
          Go ahead, captain, I'll walk.

The car drives away.

                    (CONTINUED)

79

CONTINUED:

                         KNOX (CONT' D)
          Of course I know you! From the
          first time I saw you, I knew you
          had a wonderful soul.

                         CHRIS
          Just like that?! You just knew?

                         KNOX
          Of course just like that. That's
          how you always know when it's
          right.

                         CHRIS
          And if it so happens that you're
          wrong? If it just so happens that I
          could care less about you?

                         KNOX
          Then you wouldn't be here warning
          me about Chet.

This gives Chris pause.

                         CHRIS
          Look, I've got to go. I'm gonna be
          late for the play.

                         KNOX
          Are you going with Chet?

                         CHRIS
          Chet to a play? Are you kidding?

                         KNOX
          Then let's go together.

                         CHRIS
          Knox, you are so infuriating!

                         KNOX
          Just give me one chance. If you
          don't like me after tonight, I'll
          stay away forever.

                         CHRIS
          Uh-huh.

                         KNOX
          I promise. Dead Poets honor. Come
          with me tonight, then if you don't
          want to see me again, I swear I'll
          bow out.

                         (CONTINUED)

80

CONTINUED: (2)

                         CHRIS
          God, if Chet found out he'd...

                         KNOX
          Chet won't know anything. We'll sit
          in back and sneak away as soon as
          it's over.

                         CHRIS
          Knox, if you promise that this will
          be the end of it...

                         KNOX
          Dead Poets honor.

                         CHRIS
          What is that?

                         KNOX
          My word.

He crosses his heart with his fingers and looks sincere.
Chris thinks then offers him her hand.

                         CHRIS
          You are so infuriating.

Knox smiles and does a little jig. They walk off together.

STAGE AND AUDITORIUM

High school age actors are on stage, performing "A
Midsummer Night's Dream." In the audience, the boys of the
Dead Poets Society sit with Mr. Keating. Knox enters with
Chris and they take seats. A couple of his friends shoot
him gestures of encouragement.

Neil makes his entrance. As Puck, he wears a crown of
flowers and twigs. The members of the Dead Poets Society
cheer loudly.

THE STAGE - SAME

                         NEIL (AS PUCK)
          "Thou speakest aright: I am that
          merry wanderer of the night. I jest
          to Oberon and make him smile When I
          a fat and bean-fed horse beguile,
          Neighing in likeness of a filly
          foal..."

                         (CONTINUED)

81

CONTINUED: (3)

ANGLE ON THE "DEAD POETS"

Intently watching the show. As Neil delivers his lines, getting laughs in the right places, Charlie leans to Keating.

                    CHARLIE
                (excited whisper)
        He's good! He's god damned good!

Keating answers with a thumbs up as Neil continues with the scene.

                    DISSOLVE TO:

THE PLAY

On stage are the characters of Lysander and Hermia.

                    LYSANDER
            One turf shall serve as pillow for
            us both, One heart, one bed, two
            bosoms, and one troth.

                    HERMIA
            Nay good Lysander. For my sake, my
            dear, Lie further off yet; do not
            lie so near.

ANGLE IN THE WINGS

As Hermia and Lysander play their scene, Neil stands in the wings looking out. He spots his friends in the audience and smiles. He turns and sees his father enter the rear of the auditorium and stand in the back. Neil is stunned.

ON STAGE

                    LYSANDER
            Here is my bed. Sleep give thee all
            his rest!

                GINNY (AS HERMIA)
            With half that wish the wisher's
            eyes be pressed!

BACK STAGE

Neil is still in shock over the fact that his father is here. Behind him one of his fellow actors hands him his puck crown.

                    (CONTINUED)

82

CONTINUED: (4)

                    ACTOR
                (loud whisper)
        Neil. That's your cue. Come on,
        Neil.

Neil backs into the wings and hurries to make his next
entrance.

                    DISSOLVE TO:

A MUSICAL INTERLUDE

A small musical accompaniment sits beside the stage.
Panpipes, triangle, and bongos weave a haunting spell. In
SLOW MOTION, without words, we watch Neil on stage,
playing Puck. Neil moves in a lyrical revelry,
unblushingly joyful, enchanted and enchanting. It is Neil
in the full flower of his youth.

The other characters appear in this slow motion interlude
too... Keating, Todd, and the boys awed and delighted by
everything they see. Knox stares at Chris in complete
rapture. Chris is starting to be caught up with Knox,
though she tries hard not to show it. Slowly Knox reaches
out and takes her hand. She lets him.

                    DISSOLVE TO:

THE STAGE

The interlude is over. Neil stands on stage alone as Puck.
He addresses the audience but these next words are
particularly for his father.

                    NEIL (AS PUCK)
        If we shadows have offended, Think
        but this and all is mended-- That
        you have but slumb'red here While
        these visions did appear. And this
        weak and idle theme, No more
        yielding but a dream, Gentle, do
        no reprehend. If you pardon, we
        will mend. And as I am an honest
        Puck, If we have unearned luck Now
        to scrape the serpent's tongue.
        We will make amends ere long; Else
        the Puck a liar call. So, good
        night unto you all. Give me your
        hands, if we be friends, And Robin
        shall restore amends.

                    (CONTINUED)

83

CONTINUED: (5)

If there were any doubts about Neil's talent as an actor,
they are gone. The curtain falls. The audience breaks into
enthusiastic applause.

ANGLE ON THE AUDIENCE

The boys, Keating, everybody, rising to a standing
ovation.

ANGLE ON THE STAGE AND AUDIENCE

Neil re-enters and takes his bow. The members of the Dead
Poets Society cheer. Neil bows. There are more cheers from
other members of the audience, including Keating.

INT. THE BOYS' BACKSTAGE DRESSING ROOM - SAME

The excited actors enter, jubilant about how well the play
went. Neil, in a daze, is congratulated by his fellow
actors. After a moment of celebration, the Director enters
looking worried. She speaks a low tone to Neil.

                    DIRECTOR
          Neil. Your father.

Neil nods.

INT. AUDITORIUM AND STAGE - SAME

The auditorium has cleared out except for Mr. Perry.

Putting on his coat, Neil enters the stage from the wings.
He sees his father standing at the back of the auditorium.
Neil smiles but the stern look on his father's face causes
Neil's smile to disappear. Neil steps off the stage and
approaches his father.

EXT./INT. THE AUDITORIUM LOBBY - SAME

Keating and Neil's friends are waiting in the lobby for
Neil. Suddenly Mr. Perry leads Neil like a prisoner out of
the auditorium and through the lobby. People yell
congratulations at Neil. Todd is behind the throng, trying
to reach his friend.

                    TODD
          Neil, that was great! Neil!

                    KNOX
          We're having a party!

                    (CONTINUED)

84

CONTINUED:

                         NEIL
            It's no use. I can't.

Mr. Keating reaches Neil and takes him by the shoulders.

                         KEATING
            Neil, you were brilliant!

Mr. Perry pushes Keating's hands away.

                         MR. PERRY
            Keep away from my son.

This stuns everybody. Mr. Perry leads Neil outside to his
waiting car and puts him in. As Mr. Perry walks around to
his side of the car, Charlie starts to go outside. Keating
stops Charlie.

                         KEATING
            Don't make it any worse than it is.

Mr. Perry starts the car and pulls off. Neil's face
through the window is like a prisoner being taken to his
execution.

Stunned, the members of the Dead Poets Society gather.
Charlie walks to Mr. Keating.

                         CHARLIE
            Is it okay if we walk back?
            Captain?

                         KEATING
            Sure.

The boys walk away. Keating stands, thinking.

INT. MR. PERRY'S STUDY

Neil's mother sits in the corner of the room, her eyes red
from crying. Neil's father leads in Neil who is still
wearing his Puck costume. He looks at his crying mother.
He starts to speak, then:

                         MR. PERRY
            Son, I am trying very hard to
            understand why you insist on
            defying us, but, whatever the
            reason, I am not going to let you
            ruin your life.
                    (more)

                    (CONTINUED)

85

CONTINUED:

                    MR. PERRY (Cont'd)
        Tomorrow I am withdrawing you from
        Welton and enrolling you in Braden
        Military School. You are going to
        Harvard and you are going to be a
        doctor.

Fresh tears well in Neil's already bloodshot eyes.

                    NEIL
                (pleading)
        Father, that's ten more years.
        That's a lifetime!

                  MR. PERRY
        You have opportunities I never
        dreamed of! I won't let you
        squander them.

                    NEIL
        But I have to tell you what I
        think!

                  MR. PERRY
        Then tell me. What?! Is it more of
        this acting business? Because you
        can forget that.

Neil looks at his father. He wants to speak but he sees
that it is futile.

                  MR. PERRY
        Tell me. Tell me.

                    NEIL
        Nothing?

                  MR. PERRY
        Nothing.

He looks at his wife then back to Neil.

                  MR. PERRY
        Nothing? Then let's go to bed.

Mr. Perry walks out of the room. Neil's mother looks like
she's going to say something, then doesn't. She stops
beside her son and puts her hand on his shoulder.

                    NEIL
        I was good, mother. I was really
        good.

                  (CONTINUED)

86

CONTINUED: (2)

She pats her son on the shoulder.

                    MRS. PERRY
          Go to bed.

She exits. Neil sits alone.

INT. THE PERRY'S BEDROOM - NIGHT.

Mr. and Mrs. Perry prepare for bed. They arrange their
robes and slippers then lie down. After Mr. Perry turns
out the light, we hear Mrs. Perry sobbing.

                    MR. PERRY
                    (softly)
          It's going to be all right.

INT. NEIL'S ROOM AT HIS PARENTS' HOUSE - NIGHT

Neil stands alone in his darkened room staring out the
window. The emotion is dried and gone from him, and all
feeling is drained from his face.

INT. THE HALLWAY IN NEIL'S HOUSE - NIGHT

The door to Neil's room opens and Neil walks into the
hall. He turns a corner and moves off.

INT. MR. PERRY'S STUDY - NIGHT

Moonlight illuminates the room. Neil walks to his father's
desk. He opens the top drawer and reaches in the back, and
pulls out a key. With this, he unlocks the bottom drawer
of the desk.   From this he removes a revolver.

INT. MR. PERRY'S BEDROOM - NIGHT

The CAMERA DOLLIES SLOWLY in on Mr. and Mrs. Perry as they
sleep soundly in their beds. The DOLLY comes to a stop on
the face of Mr. Perry. He suddenly sits up.

                    MR. PERRY
          What was that?

                    MRS. PERRY
          What?

                         (CONTINUED)

87

CONTINUED:

                    MR. PERRY
          That sound. Didn't you hear it?

                    MRS. PERRY
          What sound?

Mr. Perry gets out of bed.

INT. THE HALLWAY IN NEIL'S HOUSE - NIGHT

Mr. Perry, in his pajamas, strides through the hallway of
his house. He enters Neil's room, then comes back out into
the hall. He heads toward the study. Behind him, putting
on her robe, follows Mrs. Perry.

INT. MR. PERRY'S STUDY - NIGHT

Mr. Perry comes in and turns on the light. All seems
normal. He's about to leave when his attention is caught
by a black object on the carpet... a revolver. Alarmed, he
moves around to the back of the desk. He sees a pale white
hand and gasps.

                    MR. PERRY
          No!

Mr. Perry kneels down and embraces his son. Mrs. Perry
wails a horrible wail.

INT. TODD'S DORM ROOM - MORNING

The door opens and in come Charlie, Knox, and Meeks. They
look shaken. They gently wake Todd.

                    CHARLIE
          Todd. Todd...

Todd opens his eyes. He sits up, looking exhausted. His
eyes adjust to the light, then he closes them and lies
back down. He picks up his clock, squints at it.

                    TODD
          Jesus, Charlie, I gotta sleep.

He lies back down for a moment, then opens his eyes again.
He sees the other boys, standing there, staring at him. He
senses that something is wrong. He sits up.

                    CHARLIE
          Neil's dead. He shot himself.

88

EXT. WELTON, DAY.

The day is overcast and bleak. Todd shuffles across the grounds like he doesn't know who he is. His friends follow. Suddenly Todd vomits. Tears stream down his face.

> TODD
> Someone has to know it was his father! Neil wouldn't kill himself! He loved living!

> KNOX
> You don't seriously think his father...

> TODD
> Not with the gun! Damn it, even if the bastard didn't pull the trigger he--

Todd sobs. Finally he controls himself.

> TODD (CONT'D)
> Even if Mr. Perry didn't shoot him, he killed him. They have to know that!

He runs across the campus.

> TODD (CONT'D)
> NEIL! NEIL!!!

INT. KEATING'S CLASSROOM - DAY

Keating is sitting alone at his desk in the empty classroom, struggling to hold back emotion. He stands and walks slowly to Neil's desk. He picks up a book, prominent there:

It's his own battered, dog-eared, poetry anthology. He opens it. Prominent are the words on the flyleaf: "Dead Poets".

Keating sits heavily into Neil's chair. From his throat comes a sound of utter anguish.

INT. THE CHAPEL - LATER

The entire school is assembled. All finish singing a hymn then Nolan takes the podium.

89

CONTINUED:

                    NOLAN
          Gentlemen, the death of Neil Perry
          is a tragedy. He was a fine
          student, one of Welton's best, and
          he will be missed. We have
          contacted each of your parents to
          explain the situation. Naturally,
          all are quite concerned. At the
          request of Neil's family, I intend
          to conduct a thorough inquiry into
          this matter. Your complete
          cooperation is expected.

INT. THE TRUNK ROOM - DAY.

Charlie, Todd, Knox, and Pitts stand waiting in this junk-
filled room where the suitcases are stored. There is a
knock on the door, then Meeks enters.

                    MEEKS
          I can't find him.

                    CHARLIE
          You told him about this meeting?

                    MEEKS
          Twice.

                    CHARLIE
          That's it, guys, we're all fried.

                    PITTS
          What do you mean?

                    CHARLIE
          Cameron's a fink! He's in Nolan's
          office right now, finking!

                    PITTS
          About what?

                    CHARLIE
          The club, Pitts. Think about it.

Pitts and the others look bewildered.

                    CHARLIE
          They need a scapegoat. Schools go
          under because of things like this.

The trunk room door opens. Cameron enters. He sees
Charlie, Todd, Knox, Pitts, and Meeks staring at him.

                    (CONTINUED)

90

CONTINUED:

                    CAMERON
          What's going on, guys?

                    CHARLIE
          You finked, didn't you, Cameron?

                    CAMERON
          Finked? I don't know what you're
          talking about.

                    CHARLIE
          You just told Nolan everything
          about the club is what I'm talking
          about!

                    CAMERON
          In case you hadn't heard, Dalton,
          there's something called an Honor
          Code at this school. If a teacher
          asks you something, you tell the
          truth or you're expelled.

Charlie moves at Cameron.

                    CHARLIE
          Why you...

Meeks and Knox restrain Charlie.

                    KNOX
          Charlie...

                    CHARLIE
          He's a rat! He's in up to his eyes
          so he ratted to save himself!

                    KNOX
          Don't touch him, Charlie. You do
          and you're out!

                    CHARLIE
          I'm out anyway!

                    KNOX
          You don't know that. Not yet!

                    CAMERON
          He's right there, Charlie. And, if
          you're smart, every one of you will
          do exactly what I did and
          cooperate. They're not after us.
          We're the victims. Us and Neil.

                    (CONTINUED)

91

CONTINUED: (2)

                         CHARLIE
            What does that mean? Who are they
            after?

                         CAMERON
            Why, Mr. Keating, of course. The
            "Captain" himself. You didn't
            really think he could avoid
            responsibility, did you?

                         CHARLIE
            Mr. Keating? Responsible for Neil?
            Is that what they're saying?!

He pulls himself free of Meeks and Knox's grips.

                         CAMERON
            Who else do you think, dumb ass?
            The administration? Mr. Perry?
            Keating put us up to all this crap,
            didn't he? If it wasn't for him,
            Neil would be cozied up in his room
            right now, studying his chemistry
            and dreaming of being called
            doctor.
                         TODD
            That's not true! Mr. Keating didn't
            tell Neil what to do. Neil loved
            acting.

                         CAMERON
            Believe what you want, but I say
            let Keating fry. Why ruin our
            lives?

                         CHARLIE
            YOU...

Charlie bolts across the room and strikes Cameron across
the face. Cameron falls to the floor. Charlie stands over
him.

                         KNOX
            Charlie!

                         CAMERON
                 (at Charlie)
            You just signed your expulsion
            papers, "Nuwanda."

Cameron covers his bleeding nose. Charlie turns and walks
out. The others walk out too.

                         (CONTINUED)

92

CONTINUED: (3)

                    CAMERON (CONT'D)
                (shouting after them)
          If you guys are smart, you'll do
          exactly what I did! They know
          everything anyway. You can't save
          Keating but you can save
          yourselves!

INT. TODD'S DORM ROOM, DAY

Neil's bed is stripped and his desk is empty. Todd stands
at his window, looking across the campus at the
administration building. Momentarily, Meeks is escorted
out by Dr. Hager. Hager escorts Meeks across campus, back
to the dorm.

INT. THE DORM HALLWAY - SAME

Todd peers out of the door of his room. Meeks and Hager
enter the hallway. Hager stops at the end of the hall.

Meeks walks silently back to his room. As he passes Todd,
he doesn't look at him. Meeks enters his room and shuts
the door.

                    HAGER
          Knox Overstreet.

Knox comes out of his room and joins Hager at the end of
the hall. The pair exit together. Momentarily, Todd walks
across the hall to Meeks' room. Todd knocks.

                    TODD
          Meeks, it's Todd.

                    MEEKS (FROM WITHIN)
          Go away, I have to study.

Todd pauses, realizing what has happened.

                    TODD
          What happened to Nuwanda?

                    MEEKS (FROM WITHIN)
          Expelled.

Todd stands stunned.

                    TODD
          What'd you tell them?

                              (CONTINUED)

93

CONTINUED:

> MEEKS (FROM WITHIN)
> Nothing they didn't already know.

Todd turns away.

> DR. HAGER (V.O.)
> Todd Anderson.

INT. THE WELTON ACADEMY HONOR ROOM, DAY

This is the room with the staircase that leads up to
Nolan's office. Hager following, Todd climbs up the stairs
like a man climbing the gallows.

INT. MR. NOLAN'S OFFICE - DAY

Headmaster Nolan sits at his desk. Nearby are Todd's
parents. Todd enters with Dr. Hager and sees his parents.
Todd's lip starts to quiver.

> TODD
> Dad... Mom.

> NOLAN
> Have a seat, Mr. Anderson.

There is an empty chair--like the prisoner's chair at an
inquisition--in front of Nolan's desk. Todd sits. He looks
at his parents who sit steely eyed. Perspiration breaks
out all across Todd's brow.

> NOLAN (CONT' D)
> Mr. Anderson, I think we've pretty
> well put together what's happened
> here. You do admit to being a part
> of this Dead Poets Society?

Todd looks at his parents and Nolan. He closes his eyes.
He starts to nod yes. Before he can, his father speaks.

> MR. ANDERSON
> Answer him.

> TODD
> Yes...Yes sir.

Nolan holds up a piece of paper.

(CONTINUED)

94

CONTINUED:

                         NOLAN
            I have here a detailed description
            of what went on at your meetings.
            It describes how your teacher, Mr.
            Keating, encouraged you boys to
            organize the club and to use it as
            a source of inspiration for
            reckless, self-indulgent behavior.
            It describes how Mr. Keating, both
            in and out of the classroom,
            encouraged Neil Perry to follow
            this obsession with acting when he
            knew it went directly against the
            explicit orders of Neil's parents.
            It is Mr. Keating's blatant abuse
            of his position as a teacher that
            led directly to Neil Perry's death.

Nolan hands the paper to Todd.

                         NOLAN (CONT'D)
            Read this carefully, Todd. If you
            have nothing to add or amend, sign
            it.

Todd takes this paper and reads it. He spends a long time
doing so and, by the time he finishes, his hands and the
paper are shaking. Todd looks up.

                         TODD
                   (to Nolan, with great
                    difficulty speaking)
            What... what is going to
            happen...to Mr. Keating?

                         MR. ANDERSON
            Sign the paper, Todd.

                         TODD
            But...

                         MR. ANDERSON
            Sign the paper, Todd.

Nolan holds out the pen for Todd.

EXT. WELTON MAIN LAWN - DAY

The ground is covered with snow. McAllister walks across
the lawn with several boys, talking Latin. He stops and
looks up. He sees:

95

EXT. KEATING'S ROOM - DAY

The lonely figure of Mr. Keating standing in the window of
his room, looking down at McAllister. Their eyes lock
momentairly then:

EXT. WELTON MAIN LAWN - DAY

McAllister's eyes turn away. He takes a deep breath then
resumes with the boys.

INT. KEATING'S DORM ROOM - SAME

Keating moves away from his window. He starts to take down
his beloved books of poetry - his Byron, his Whitman, his
Wordsworth - then he leaves them. He closes his suitcase.

INT. THE ENGLISH CLASSROOM - DAY

Todd, Knox, Meeks, Pitts, Cameron and the rest of the
class are there. Conspicuously empty are Neil's desk and
Charlie's desk. Todd looks numb, his gaze downward,
reminding us of the way he looked when we first met him.
Knox, Meeks, and Pitts look humiliated. All of the former
club members are too ashamed of themselves to look at one
another. Only Cameron looks halfway normal. He sits
studying at his desk as though nothing has happened.

The door opens. In strides Mr. Nolan. All stand. Nolan
sits at the teacher's desk. All sit down.

                    NOLAN
          I will be taking over this class
          through exams. We will find a
          permanent English teacher during
          the break. Who will tell me where
          you are in the Pritchard textbook?

Nolan looks around. There are no volunteers.

                    NOLAN (CONT'D)
          Mr. Anderson?

                    TODD
          (softly, barely audible)
          The... Pritchard...

Todd looks through his books. He fumbles nervously.

                    NOLAN
          I can't hear you, Mr. Anderson.
          Kindly tell me, Mr. Cameron.

                    (CONTINUED)

96

CONTINUED:

                    CAMERON
          We skipped around a lot, sir. We
          covered the romantics and some of
          the chapters on post Civil War
          literature.

                    NOLAN
          What about the realists?

                    CAMERON
          I believe we skipped most of that.

Nolan stares at Cameron and the class.

                    NOLAN
          All right then, we'll start over.
          What is poetry?

Nolan waits for an answer. No one volunteers. The door to
the classroom opens. Mr. Keating enters.

                    KEATING
                (to Nolan)
          I came for my personals. Should I
          come back after class?

                    NOLAN
          Get them now, Mr. Keating.
                (to the class)
          Gentlemen, turn to page 21 of the
          introduction. Mr. Cameron, read
          aloud the excellent essay by Dr.
          Pritchard on Understanding Poetry.

                    CAMERON
          Mr. Nolan, that page has been
          ripped out.

                    NOLAN
          Then borrow somebody else's book.

                    CAMERON
          They're all ripped out, sir.

                    NOLAN
          What do you mean they're all ripped
          out?

                    CAMERON
          Sir, we...

                    NOLAN
          Never mind, Cameron.

                         (CONTINUED)

97

CONTINUED: (2)

Nolan carries his textbook to Cameron's desk.

> NOLAN (CONT'D)
> Read.

> CAMERON
> "Understanding Poetry by Dr. J.
> Evans Pritchard, Ph.D. To fully
> understand poetry, we must first be
> fluent with its meter, rhyme, and
> figures of speech, then ask two
> questions: 1) how artfully has the
> objective...

As Cameron continues reading, Keating, who is in the
anteroom collecting his things, looks out at the students.
He sees Todd, whose eyes are near tears. He sees Knox,
Meeks, Pitts... still too ashamed to look him in the eye,
but nevertheless full of emotion. The irony of Nolan
choosing the Pritchard essay is too incredible.

Keating finishes his packing. He walks back into the
classroom and crosses towards the door. Just as Keating
reaches the door, Todd can no longer hold in what he is
feeling. Todd stands.

> TODD
> (interrupting Cameron's
> reading)
> Mr. Keating, they made everybody
> sign it!

> NOLAN
> Quiet, Mr. Anderson!

> TODD
> Mr. Keating, it's true! You have to
> believe me.

> KEATING
> I believe you, Todd.

> NOLAN
> Leave, Mr. Keating!

> TODD
> But it wasn't his fault, Mr. Nolan!

Nolan strides down the aisle and pushes Todd back into his
seat.

(CONTINUED)

98

CONTINUED: (3)

                    NOLAN
        Sit down, Mr. Anderson! One more
        outburst from you—
              (turns to the class)
        Or anyone else! And you are out of
        this school!

He turns toward Keating, who has taken a few steps back
toward Todd, as though to help.

                    NOLAN
            Leave, Mr. Keating!

The boys stare at Keating. He stares at them, taking them
in for the last time.

                    NOLAN
        I said leave, Mr. Keating.

Keating turns and walks toward the door.

                    TODD
        Oh Captain, my captain!

Keating turns to look at Todd. So does everybody else.
Todd props one foot up on his desk, then stands up on it.
He stands atop his desk, holding back tears, facing Mr.
Keating.

                    NOLAN
              (moving at Todd)
        Sit down!

As Nolan moves down the aisle toward Todd, Knox (whose
seat is on the other side of the room) calls Mr. Keating's
name and stands up on his desk too. Nolan turns and sees
this. Meeks musters his courage and stands on his desk.
Pitts does the same. One by one and then in groups, many
others in the class follow suit, standing on their desks
in salute to Mr. Keating.

Nolan, who started at Todd, then at Knox, stands
motionless. He is amazed by this overwhelming response.

Keating stands at the door, overcome with emotion.

                    KEATING
        Thank you, boys. ...Thank you.

Keating looks into Todd's eyes, then into all their eyes.

ANGLE ON the members of the Dead Poets Society standing on
their desks:

                                        (CONTINUED)

99

CONTINUED: (4)

MEEKS

PITTS

KNOX

and finally, TODD, who is holding back tears but standing proud.

BLACKOUT.